A Fairy Tale Affair

How to Plan a Fabulous
Destination
Wedding
on a Shoestring Budget

Deborah McKenzie & Danielle Wigfall

Self-published with CreateSpace

Nonfiction / Reference / Wedding Planning / Destination Weddings

ISBN-13: 978-1497586369
ISBN-10: 1497586364

Cover design by Tyson Wigfall
Interior technical formatting by Lee Reed, III

A Fairy Tale Affair

To: _____

From: _____

Message: _____

_____

_____

Table of Contents

Introduction   vi

     Mother-of-the-Bride Perspective

     Bride Perspective

1. Why a Destination Wedding Could be Right for You   9
2. Choosing a Location   13
3. Destination Jamaica   21
4. Destination Dominican Republic   29
5. Destination Mexico   37
6. Destination Bahamas   45
7. Destination Saint Lucia   51
8. Destination Costa Rica   57
9. Destination Las Vegas and Cruise Ships   63
10. Selecting a Date   69
11. Select and Invite your Attendants   73
12. First Things First – Legalities/Contracts   79
13. Guest List   85
14. Creating Your Wedding Website   89
15. Creating your Wedding Program and Name Cards   91
16. Wedding Theme, Colors and Attire   95
17. Wedding Day Prep and Packing   99
18. Wedding Week Activities   103
19. Welcome Letter and Gift Bags   111
20. The Wedding Ceremony   115
21. The Reception and Honeymoon   121
22. Traditions, T-shirts and Thank you's   125
23. Directory and Resources   128

Introduction

Mother-of-the-Bride Perspective:

As a mother of a bride-to-be, I was completely lost when we started planning my daughter's destination wedding. We initially started out by hiring a wedding planner for destination weddings. We chose what appeared to be a very professional company. However, after our planner missed some key follow-up dates, we began to question the planner's competency. We also began thinking that we were not getting anything more than what we could have done ourselves with time and some research, *for free.* After paying a deposit and other additional costs, we ended up terminating our contract with the wedding planner. We summed it up as a lesson learned.

Having lost time, in addition, to our deposit, we felt a bit stressed at that moment. Although, both my daughter and I had professional event planning experience, we had no experience planning a destination wedding.

We did what most 21st century people do when they have a question. We went to the Internet. Although we were able to find some information, there was not a single source that provided the answers to most of our questions. We then looked for books and magazines with a focus on planning a destination wedding. We thought surely, with the popularity of destination weddings, we would find a "how-to" book that would answer most of our questions, and guide us toward planning a fabulous destination wedding. To our surprise, there weren't many books on the topic.

Yes, there were many books and resources devoted to planning a wedding, but not many resources or books that focused specifically on destination weddings. What we were able to find, although helpful, still fell short of answering many questions that we had. Also, because of our experience in event planning, we felt that many details that could have been included in some of the resources that we reviewed; were left out. We had also developed some excellent original ideas of our own.

That is when we decided that we would plan the event ourselves! This decision not only saved us thousands of dollars, but my daughter ended up having an absolutely Fabulous Destination Wedding (FDW)... *A Fairy Tale Affair.*

Bride's Perspective:

If you would have told me when I became engaged that I would have a Fabulous Destination Wedding the next year, I would have laughed and thought only in my dreams. I knew absolutely nothing about destination weddings besides the fact that they involved traveling to exotic and luxurious locations. I didn't know anyone who had a destination wedding, especially at my age and I thought it would be too expensive to even consider.

The road to my FDW began when I was trying to find the perfect venue for our wedding. With my husband's family residing on the east coast, my family in the mid-west and us living in California I searched from coast to coast. If half or the majority of our family and friends were going to have to travel anyway, then in essence, we were already having a destination wedding from our guests' perspective. As it turned out, our friends and family that lived locally were all too ready to jet out to a fabulous destination if we could plan it on a cost-friendly budget. Having a Fabulous Destination Wedding was the perfect option!

I couldn't believe it; I was soon planning my own Fabulous Destination Wedding, however, we only had a shoestring budget. There's a saying that, "you either spend time or spend money", we didn't have money, so after terminating our contract with a destination wedding planner, we spent our time researching and planning. In the end, we could not have had a more Fabulous Destination Wedding, even if we had spent thousands more.

Having a destination wedding was one of the best decisions I've ever made. When done right, you can really have an unbelievable wedding. I was shocked to find out that many of my friends who didn't attend the wedding thought my pictures were backdrops.

Several people who actually watched the ceremony from their balconies approached me throughout the rest of the week with overwhelming amounts of love and flattering remarks about the wedding. One woman approached me crying while expressing how beautiful the wedding was. I had no idea how much our wedding affected everyone. Every one of my guests had an amazing time and still talk about it. It brings so much joy to hear the family reminisce about all the fun and funny experiences from one of the best times in their lives. Our special day wasn't just special to us, but to all of the guests that enjoyed it with us!

After planning my own destination wedding I was approached by several friends and acquaintances to plan and coordinate their weddings and destination weddings. One of my guests was so inspired by my destination wedding that she decided to have one as well. In less than a year after my own wedding, she was tying the knot on an exotic island. Next thing I know, I am now coordinating and planning weddings and special events for local couples and even some celebrities. It's so inspiring to dream, but even more exciting when your dreams come true.

Chapter 1 Why a Destination Wedding Could be Right for You

If you are reading this book, then you, most likely, are newly-engaged and planning one of the most important days of your life – your wedding day! Right now, you are probably wondering if a destination wedding is right for you. Is it more complicated to plan? Will people come? What about the weather? Will the marriage be legal? And most importantly, how much will it cost?

This book will answer these questions and more while guiding you toward having a Fabulous Destination Wedding (FDW) on a shoestring budget. Since this book focuses on destination weddings, it can be used independently, or as a companion book to your other wedding guide books. We also have some original ideas that can be utilized in local weddings in your hometown.

Cost-effective

With a typical wedding topping $25,000, the cost for a local wedding can be budget-busting. Most couples are surprised to find out that destination weddings can actually be much cheaper than one in your hometown. Many costs associated with a destination wedding are already included in the wedding package from many all-inclusive resorts. In addition, destination weddings, generally, have shorter guest lists, so you save on per person costs.

> **FDW Tip:** The FDW team recommends that you budget expenses and allocate resources based on items that will take your wedding from typical to Fabulous. For example, an upgrade to your floral package would probably have very little impact on your special day, especially for Destination Weddings in tropical locales. So you could possibly forego a floral upgrade and help your budget.

Honeymoon is Free

A big advantage to having a destination wedding is that your honeymoon is free! If you choose to have your wedding at an all-inclusive resort, which we, the Fabulous Destination Wedding team (FDW Team) highly advises, then there are no additional costs for your honeymoon. All-inclusive resorts typically include your room, meals, drinks, and entertainment such as nightly shows. Many resorts also offer complimentary non-motorized watersports.

Why a Destination Wedding Could be Right for You

Convenience

The bride and groom do not have to travel after the ceremony to their honeymoon location. A quick elevator ride up takes them to their honeymoon suite. After the wedding, who really wants to hassle with traffic, long lines, and airport security?

Peace of Mind

Resorts and hotels host weddings on a regular basis. This is especially true for hotels and resorts that service destination weddings. With a destination wedding, resort staff and personnel understand that their clients are unfamiliar with a lot of the local wedding legal requirements; and serve as valuable resources.

Beyond Cookie-Cutter

Destination weddings, although becoming more and more popular, are still considered out of the norm. Guests who generally attend destination weddings are open to a couple stepping outside the box. Also, people feel much freer when they are on vacation, so if you want to do something unique or a little wacky, a destination wedding would be the way to go.

Cultural Interaction

Another benefit to having a destination wedding is the opportunity to experience a different culture. Some of your guests may not have taken the opportunity to travel outside the United States, if it were not for your wedding. Even today, most Americans do not have passports.

Family Reunion

Destination weddings can also serve dual-purpose as a family reunion creating great family memories. Many couples have expressed to the FDW team that their destination wedding brought their family closer by sharing extended time together and rekindling lost bonds.

Great Photo Op

With a destination wedding, there's no need to take pre-wedding pictures at your local botanic gardens, or other locale. Your destination will have many spots for great photo opportunities.

> **FDW Tip: A great photo opportunity for the bride and groom and their guests immediately follows the end of the wedding ceremony. The FDW team recommends that after the couple recesses down the aisle, with each row of guests following, that everyone line up for a group photograph with the bride and groom.**

A Fairy Tale Affair

Second Time Around / Renew Vows

Destination Weddings are also considered a top choice for couples who are getting married for the second time or renewing their wedding vows. After having a traditional ceremony, many couples decide that they want something different the second time around, so they opt for a destination wedding.

Sentimental

What is more sentimental than going back to the location that you were married at for a special anniversary? By having a destination wedding, couples have the opportunity to visit the place where their life together officially began. That destination will always be extra-special for the couple. It will also always be extra-special for the guests, too. Most guests remember the destination weddings they attend, while soon forgetting weddings held locally.

Still not convinced if a destination wedding is right for you?

- Do you want to have a fabulous fairy tale affair, but only have a beer budget? Or maybe you have the money for a champagne affair, but would rather spend it on life after the wedding?

- Are your family and friends spread out across the country, so that even if you were to have a wedding in your hometown, it would still be a destination wedding from your guests' perspective?

- Are many of your friends getting married, and you have had your share of baked chicken, typical wedding music and conversation? Do you want your special day to be just that, special?

- Have you always been the one-in-a-crowd that stood out; with your friends always anticipating, but never quite knowing what you would do next?

- Or do you consider yourself conservative, and want to step out of your comfort zone?

- Maybe you just want a Fabulous Destination Wedding on some tropical island with water adventures from parasailing to kayaking by day, and the sounds of the ocean by night?

Then a destination wedding could be right for you!

Chapter 2   Choosing a Location

YES, you can have a Fabulous Destination Wedding on a shoestring budget! Do you have dreams of saying your I-dos on the beachfront of a tropical island amongst a backdrop of palm trees and thatched huts, while listening to the rhythmic sounds of the ocean? That is the vision that most people have when they think about destination weddings. For many couples, that vision is outside of the scope of reality, for them. However, with proper research, organization and planning it not only is possible, but typically, it is cheaper than having a local wedding.

The one item that will have the most impact on your wedding and reception is your location. More than any other factor, the location sets the tone for the event. With a destination wedding the "wow" factor is automatically built in. Not only does your location set the tone for your wedding and reception, it also dictates the cost. Couples are surprised to find out that with destination weddings, location is where the biggest savings occurs. Sure, there are ways to save on expenses when having a typical local wedding, however, why have "typical" when you can have "fabulous"?

The primary reason why couples are able to cut costs with a destination wedding is because fewer guests are able to attend. Instead of having a guest list including everyone that are friends with you on Facebook, along with your second cousin twice removed, the people that will actually attend, genuinely have a connection with you.

Simply stated, the cost of catering a reception for 50 guests is, generally, 75% less than the cost of 200 guests. Doing the math, at $50 per head, a wedding of 200 guests would cost $10,000, just for catering, versus, $2500 for 50 guests. That's a possible savings of $7500 just by choosing to have a fabulous destination wedding! And that's just the beginning of the savings opportunities possible by choosing to have a destination wedding.

You may be asking yourself, "What about the cost of your guests traveling to your destination wedding?" Unless you are the son or daughter of a billionaire; guests understand and accept that they incur the costs of traveling to a destination wedding.

It is also understood, that their presence is their gift. Although some guests that attend, will also give a gift, usually monetary. Of course, gifts will still be given by friends and family that are unable to attend. It would be appropriate to register with a bridal registry for guests that are unable to attend your destination wedding.

Group Discounts Offered

Most hotels and resorts also offer group rates for guests, and discounts or upgrades to the bride and groom based on how many guests will be booking rooms at that hotel. This is an additional savings for the bride and groom. If the couple were planning an out-of-town honeymoon anyway, by having a destination wedding, you can possibly save on your room rate. If you do receive a discount or upgrade based on the number of people that book at that hotel or resort; it may be best to keep that information private. It would not be unheard of to have a savings of $200 to $500 or more on your hotel room costs.

Costs of Airfare/Travel

The cost of airfare to your destination wedding or honeymoon location could be expensive, as well, depending on your location. Since you will be combining your wedding, reception and honeymoon all in one place, you do save some costs here; however, you may need to compromise on the location of your destination wedding in order to keep costs as low as possible. Also, more of your guests will be able to attend, if the cost of attending is reasonable.

Although the South Pacific may be one of your dream vacation destinations, you would need to research the costs of having a destination wedding there, if you only have a shoestring budget. When choosing the location of your destination wedding, research the costs of traveling from your hometown to the different destinations that you are considering. This could be a savings of $500 to $1000 or more in travel expenses

Travel Advisory

When traveling, upon re-entering the United States by air, all citizens, regardless of their age, must show a U.S. passport in book format.

For U.S. citizens, it is recommended that you sign up online with the Smart Traveler Enrollment Program (STEP). A Smart Traveler app is also available for download for travel information. Visit the U.S. Department of State, Bureau of Consular Affairs website at http://travel.state.gov/ for travel advice and information.

Time of Year

Time of travel will have a major impact on your travel expenses and your destination of choice. Although June is considered the preferred month for wedding nuptials, June can also be one of the most expensive months, especially for a destination wedding. For the purposes of travel, the year is divided into 3 seasons: peak, off-peak and shoulder. Supply and demand is what drives the costs of travel. Weather conditions are the main criteria that differentiate between the travel seasons for a locale.

Generally speaking, **peak season** runs mid-June through August. When planning a FDW on a shoestring budget, typically peak season will not be an option. However, don't totally rule out peak season, you may just luck up on an unbelievable deal, or you may not have a choice.

Off-peak is typically considered the months of November through March. Hurricane season, which impacts travel to the Caribbean, Mexico and Florida, is also off-peak travel times. The Atlantic Hurricane season is from June 1st through November 30th.

August through October are the most active months for hurricanes, according to the Atlantic Oceanographic and Meteorological Laboratory (AOML). Hurricane season is very risky, especially for destination weddings. The FDW team advises against planning a FDW in hurricane vulnerable locales during this time. Off-peak can provide the best travel deals, but shoulder season may be a better option.

Shoulder season is an excellent compromise for travelers with budgetary constraints. Shoulder season, in general, is April through Mid-June and September through October (except hurricane vulnerable locales). Also, the week following a holiday can typically be a good time to travel on a budget, especially for cruises.

> **FDW Tip:** Check with local travel bureaus and hotel personnel for weather conditions and travel advisories when researching your destination options. You will also want to inquire about peak, off-peak and shoulder season since it varies by destination.

Proximity to Airport and Attractions

Also, when choosing a location, give consideration to the proximity of the hotel and resort to the airport and tourist attractions. This is not just for convenience,

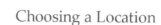

but will also keep your costs down. Hotels usually offer free shuttle service to close-by attractions and transfers to and from the airport are either free or at a small cost. If the location is further from the airport and attractions, then you and your guests will have to spend additional funds to travel to and from the airport and to the attractions. However, this expense could be offset if the resort costs and amenities or other costs make up for that difference. Again, do your research. This could be a savings of up to $100 or more on travel and transportation costs.

Legal Requirements

Another key consideration when selecting your destination wedding location are the legal requirements to obtain a marriage license in that locale. Although we will touch on this later in the book, it should be noted that some countries require residency requirements of 30 days, others have no residency requirements and you can obtain a marriage license immediately. Other requirements could be blood tests, passports, certified copy of birth certificate, translation in Spanish of all marriage documents, and possibly other requirements. Each country is unique in their specific requirements, so choosing a location with the fewest requirements may be worth the extra consideration.

Popular Destination Wedding Locations

The most popular destination wedding locations have made getting hitched in their countries simple, convenient, and budget-friendly. The tourism industry in these countries caters to the destination wedding crowd and the hotels and resorts in these countries have mostly all of your wedding details considered in their wedding packages. Although you can select to have your destination wedding in a different locale, if you truly want a hassle-free wedding, one of these destinations may be right for you. Future chapters will discuss this in more detail.

All-inclusive Resort Package

> **FDW Tip: To have a Fabulous Destination Wedding on a shoestring budget, the FDW team highly recommends that you consider an all-inclusive package or resort for your destination wedding.**

The FDW team considers selecting a hotel/resort with an all-inclusive package as a top consideration when choosing the location for your destination wedding. This decision can save you and your guests $500 – 1000 or more in food, drinks, and entertainment.

In addition, you and your guests can relax knowing that you will not have a big bill to pay at the end of your stay. Many all-inclusive resorts have a selection of restaurants, nightly entertainment and a host of activities and non-motorized water sports that are included in the package. They also typically offer a la carte amenities such as massages and motorized water sports at an additional cost.

> **FDW Tip:** Although the FDW team emphasizes all-inclusive resorts, with a little more research and planning, you open up your options to very unique, one-of-a-kind resorts and hotels. Just be sure to take into consideration all of your costs and expenses.

Wedding Packages

Be selective when choosing locations and what is offered in the hotel or resort's wedding package. Each resort varies in what they offer, and is subject to change, without notice, so be sure to read the fine print, and get all negotiated contracts in writing. Choosing a budget-friendly wedding package could be a huge savings of $250 to $2500 or more for the couple.

Basic wedding packages could include:
Minister fees
Arrangement for Marriage License and Official Certificate
Wedding Coordinator services
Wedding Dress Pressing Services
Flowers and Decorations
Pictures / Photography
Sound System and Microphone for Ceremony
Wedding Cake

> **FDW Tip:** When choosing your wedding location review and compare the different options and costs of the wedding packages offered.

Of course, the hotels and resorts will offer you the option to upgrade from their standard options.

> **FDW Tip:** The FDW team recommends ONLY considering upgrades that are extremely important to you and will have a major impact on your wedding and memories years later.

Choosing a Location

One such consideration would be to opt for videography. Although you may have friends that can take snapshots of your event, not many people are trained to take a professional video of your affair. This may be worth the cost, if not included in the wedding package.

Family-friendly vs. Adult-only

Another consideration would be choosing a hotel or resort that is aligned with your need to be family-friendly or exclusively for adults-only. If you plan to have an adult-only affair, and prefer an adults-only resort, then this would need to be taken into consideration when selecting your hotel or resort.

On the other hand, if you plan to have children attend your wedding, or have no preference, then a resort that is family-friendly may suit your tastes. If you have no preference, then a family-friendly resort will open up your options. In addition, children do tend to add additional jubilation when on vacation; even if you are watching other vacationing families with their children playing in the sand.

Other Considerations

As a couple, you may have additional considerations when selecting a location for your destination wedding. Make sure you have a list of things that are not negotiable, and be flexible on everything else. Choosing your location wisely will net the most cost savings to your wedding budget. Spend time researching and deciding on the locale, hotel or resort of your Fabulous Destination Wedding.

FDW Tip: When researching locations, the FDW team highly recommends avoiding over-researching the property. We believe the excessive review of pictures and videos can ruin the excitement when traveling. Although some couples choose to visit locations in advance, we do not recommend that either. It will take away from the surprise and wow factor when you arrive for your wedding.

Some of the top affordable destinations for weddings are:
Jamaica
Dominican Republic
Mexico
Bahamas
Saint Lucia
Costa Rica
Las Vegas

Cruise Ship

In the next several chapters, we will review these destinations. We have selected a list of destinations, based on the goal of having a Fabulous Destination Wedding on a shoestring budget. Since many factors can impact travel costs, our selections, by no means represents all the choices available. However, we do provide a good base for you to begin your research. We also have taken extra effort to highlight specific categories for these destinations, (i.e. marriage license requirements for each destination) so that you can to a quick comparison for further research.

When researching destinations, remember that a more cost-friendly location will assure that more of your family and friends will be able to attend. It is the experiences that you will share with your family and friends that will make your destination wedding fabulous and memorable for years to come.

You also have the option of having a symbolic destination wedding and legalizing it in your hometown either before or after your destination wedding. This may be a good option if you select a location that has marriage license requirements that are more stringent. Again, do your research. You can stick to your budget AND have a Fabulous Destination Wedding! Do your research and plan. Again, "you either spend time or you spend money".

Local vs. Destination Wedding

Marriage License Requirements

If you get married locally or have a destination wedding, the process for applying for a marriage license is similar. There may be a few more documents required for a destination wedding, but resorts have on-site Wedding Coordinators to assist you every step of the way. Be sure to meet the marriage license requirements either for your hometown, or far away destination wedding.

Weather Conditions

Weather conditions are a consideration for both local and destination weddings. For a hometown or destination wedding be sure to do your research when selecting your wedding date!

Chapter 3   Destination Jamaica

Why Jamaica? Jamaica will get you from A to All Right! Jamaica, a Caribbean island, is one of the most budget friendly locations for a Fabulous Destination Wedding, with its many all-inclusive resorts. The room rate for most resorts will include the room, meals, drinks, entertainment, and activities, including non-motorized water sports. Jamaica has a strong market for destination weddings, and of all the locations we will highlight, the FDW team consider that Jamaica has the easiest marriage license requirements for non-residents. Jamaica has miles upon miles of sandy beaches and untouched coastline; waterfalls that you can actually climb, natural mineral baths and of course, that famous reggae beat that will have you and your guests feeling the vibe and saying "yeah mon" by the time you leave.

Destination Highlights

Jamaica is the third largest Caribbean island. The majestic Blue Mountains dominate the inland. The most popular tourist destinations are the city and towns including **Montego Bay**, **Ocho Rios**, **Runaway Bay** and **Negril**. Jamaica is known for Bob Marley and reggae music, its vibrant culture, beautiful beaches, championship golf courses, warm people, rum and food. British author, Ian Fleming, of the James Bond series, lived on the island, and used the island as the setting of many of his novels. The actor, Errol Flynn, hosted many wild Hollywood parties on Navy Island, off the coast of **Port Antonio**, Jamaica. Visit the Jamaica Tourist Board for additional information about Jamaica.

Fun Facts

Many of the James Bond novels were written in Jamaica at "Goldeneye", a bungalow where Ian Fleming would retreat in January and February to write another book in the series.

Three of the James Bonds films have scenes that were shot in Jamaica, *Live and Let Die*, *Dr. No*, and *The Man with the Golden Gun*.

Errol Flynn is quoted for stating that Jamaica is, "more beautiful than any woman I have ever known".

The founder of Sandals Resorts International was born in Jamaica. The very first Sandals resort opened in Montego Bay, Jamaica. The rest is history.

Destination Jamaica

The film, *Cool Runnings* was inspired by Jamaica's first Winter Olympics bobsled team.

The Blue Mountains of Jamaica are named after the "blue" mists that often cover them.

Language
The official language is English.

Currency
The Jamaican dollar (J$) is the official currency; however, the American dollar is widely accepted.

Drinking Age
Drinking age in Jamaica is 18+.

Climate
Jamaica has tropical weather year round. It averages about 300 sunny days per year, with two rainy seasons.

Airports / Travel Documents Required
Jamaica has three international airports. **Sangster International Airport (MBJ)** is located in Montego Bay. **Norman Manley International Airport (KIN)** is located in the capital city of Kingston. Named after the author, the **Ian Fleming International Airport (OCJ)**, the newest, is located in Ocho Rios and also serves small aircrafts.

To travel to Jamaica you will need to have a valid passport. It is also recommended that you take an additional picture ID.

Upon re-entering the United States by air, all citizens, regardless of their age, must show a U.S. passport in book format.

For U.S. citizens, it is recommended that you sign up online with the Smart Traveler Enrollment Program (STEP). A Smart Traveler app is also available for download for travel information. Visit the U.S. Department of State, Bureau of Consular Affairs website at http://travel.state.gov/ for additional travel advice and information.

Disclaimer:

Documentation needed depends on your country of citizenship and residency. Although we do offer some information on documentation requirements, you will need to check the current entry requirements for your country of citizenship and not be dependent on the information presented here.

Montego Bay

Montego Bay, called MoBay by locals, is the second largest city in Jamaica and home to all-inclusive beachfront resorts, restaurants, shopping and attractions. Because of its close proximity to Sangster International Airport, a 10 - 15 minute cab ride to most resorts, it is a popular choice for tourists and destination weddings.

Local Attractions and Entertainment

Hip Strip is the place to experience nightlife in Montego Bay. It is a tourist destination with souvenir shops, restaurants and even has a casino. Margaritaville is one of the most popular restaurants and bars on the strip. Most resorts will offer shuttle service to and from Hip Strip.

Rose Hall Great House is allegedly the plantation home of Anne Palmer, called the "White Witch" of Jamaica. It is now open for touring and catered events.

Doctor's Cave Beach Club is world famous for the mineral content of its water and white-sand beach.

Play with the dolphins at **Dolphin Cove at Half Moon.**

Agua Sol Theme Park located on the Walter Fletcher Beach Complex offers activities including watersports, tennis courts, table tennis, and a go-cart racing course

Bamboo Rafting at Martha Brae or Mountain Valley allows you to relax as an expert guides you down the tropical riverbank. Bamboo Rafting is a favorite of Newlyweds.

Take a **Canopy Zip line Adventure Tour** through nature and see Jamaica from the rainforest.

Experience the **Luminous Lagoon** that illuminates when agitated, and watch the outline of fish as they are illuminated in the water.

Visit **Rastafari Indigenous Village** and take a guided tour through the Montego Bay River Gardens and experience Rastafari drumming, dancing, crafts and cooking.

Enjoy panoramic views of marine life by taking a **MoBay Undersea Tour.**

Take a **Chukka Jeep or ATV Safari** tour and see the natural beauty that is Jamaica.

Enjoy Asian and Caribbean cuisine to live music at one of the newest establishments, favored by celebrities, **Blue Beat**.

Ocho Rios

Ocho Rios is a town on the north coast of Jamaica, and the port-of-call for many cruise ships. It is about 1 ½ hours from Sangster International Airport.

Local Attractions and Entertainment

Climb a 600-ft waterfall at the world-renowned **Dunn's River Falls.** This is definitely one of Jamaica's treasures and a must-experience for anyone visiting Ocho Rios or one of its nearby destinations.

A must-experience is bobsledding at Mystic Mountain through **Rainforest Adventures**. Experience what it would feel like to bobsled at the Olympics, but through a rainforest!

Interact with bottlenose dolphins and other exotic wildlife including Nurse Sharks, and Stingrays at **Dolphin Cove**, Ocho Rios. It is ranked amongst the best in the world for experiencing dolphins. Kayaking, snorkeling and other activities are also offered. It is another must-experience attraction.

Take a wave runner tour on the beautiful **James Bond Beach**, located just 20 minutes from Ocho Rios and pass Golden Eye where Ian Fleming penned many James Bond novels. The beach also hosts many local and international concerts.

White sand **Reggae Beach** is located in a lush tropical jungle flanked by cliffs on either side.

Coyaba River Garden and Museum offers Jamaican Spanish architecture, waterfalls and a museum island history focusing on Taino and Arawak culture.

The Enchanted Gardens are beautiful botanical gardens set in the mountainside. A natural river creates 14 waterfalls. It also is home to a domed walk-in aviary with 80 different species of birds.

Runaway Bay

Runaway Bay is located on the north coast and 10 miles west of Ocho Rios and east of Discovery Bay. It is preferred by tourists that want to experience everything that the all-inclusive resorts have to offer and beautiful beaches with less foot traffic. It is also close to Ocho Rios and its attractions.

Local Attractions and Entertainment

Scuba dive with **Jamaica Scuba Divers Ltd.; Resort Divers and Watersports** or **ScubaQuatic Arrecife** and experience Jamaica's diverse coral reef.

A must-experience is **The Runaways Sports Bar and Grill** for excellent food and a true Jamaican experience.

Explore **Green Grotto Caves** or tour Discovery Bay Marine Laboratory in nearby Discovery Bay.

Negril

Negril's seven mile beach has been regularly rated as one of the top beaches in the world. Large, all-inclusive resorts are flanked to the north, while smaller; boutique hotels are located to the south.

Local Attractions and Entertainment

Seven Mile Beach is one of the main attractions in Negril. It offers pristine white sand and crystal clear water with jaw-dropping sunsets at night.

Negril's Cliffs is a must-experience for all travelers and could be described as paradise on earth. The sunsets are truly spectacular.

The cliff side restaurant and bar, **Rick's Café** is known for its location and spectacular sunsets. If you go to Negril, you must definitely go to Rick's Café during your trip.

Y S Falls and **Mayfield Falls** offer a jungle experience with spectacular waterfalls, and natural spring pools. The waterfalls are truly a must-experience for anyone visiting Negril.

Appleton Estate Jamaica Rum Tours will give you the opportunity to view first-hand the process of distilling rum in present day, and in years past from a company that has been in the business since the 1700s. Be sure to purchase a few souvenirs from this tourist attraction!

While visiting, be sure to check out **Negril's historic lighthouse.**

Port Antonio

Port Antonio is considered by some locals as the true, unspoiled Jamaica; a hidden gem.

Local Attractions and Entertainment

Island Routes Caribbean Adventure Tours offers many tour options from rafting to watersports, and everything in-between. Their aim is to showcase the beauty, culture and natural resources of the Caribbean Islands.

MARRIAGE LICENSE REQUIREMENTS

Getting married in Jamaica is easy and inexpensive, and only requires a 24-hour waiting period after you arrive on the island. No blood tests are required. The marriage license is valid for three months.

FDW Tip: To ensure that you are meeting the marriage license requirements for your destination wedding; it is highly recommended by the FDW team that you select a hotel or resort that has a specialty in wedding planning. You can then utilize their expertise and guidance to getting a marriage license and having a legal ceremony. Larger resorts and hotels will take care of the many details for obtaining a marriage license.

Disclaimer:

Although we offer general information for getting married in various destinations, you will need to research the requirements of your home country and selected destination for the current requirements, laws, and regulations. We provide information here on Civil Ceremonies only.

Documents Needed

- Proof of citizenship - certified copy of birth certificate
- Passport or Driver's License
- Certified Documents supporting any change in name
- Parental written consent, if under 18.
- Proof of divorce (if applicable) - certified copy or original Certificate of Divorce
- Copy of Death Certificate for widow or widower (if applicable)
- Declaration Form completed by a person with knowledge of impending marriage

Residency Requirement
24-hour waiting period after arrival to island

Marriage License
Issued by the Government of Jamaica, Ministry of Justice

Marriage License Fee
J$4000.00 or approximately US$38.00

> **FDW Tip:** Consult with your wedding coordinator at your hotel or resort, in advance, on requirements for obtaining a marriage license. Most resorts and hotels will request that you send them the documents months prior and will take care of the application process.

Ceremony

The marriage ceremony must be performed before 8:00 PM

Only a Marriage Officer licensed in Jamaica can legally marry a couple.

Witnesses

Two witnesses must be present at the ceremony and for the signing of the marriage certificate. The Marriage Officer can also serve as a witness.

Note: Much of the information provided in this section was gathered from the Tourism Board or Bureau for the location. Please see the Directory for a list of Tourism Boards and Bureaus.

Chapter 4   Destination Dominican Republic

Why the Dominican Republic? The Dominican Republic has it all. In the Dominican Republic you can design your dream vacation! Looking for a dream island paradise with amazing pristine white sand beaches? The Dominican Republic has over 250 miles of beautiful and scenic coastline waiting to enchant you. What if you want to add culture and history to the mix? Check out the city of Santo Domingo, the oldest city in the New World. What about adventure and adrenaline-rushing activities? The Dominican Republic has everything from zip-lining to scuba diving and everything in-between. It is a very popular destination for weddings and has many all-inclusive resort options available.

Destination Highlights

The Dominican Republic occupies the eastern two-thirds of the Caribbean island of Hispaniola. Its history is a mixture of European, African and native Taino Indian cultures. Popular tourist destinations include its capital city, Santo Domingo on the southern coast, the oldest city in the new world, rich in history and culture. The United Nations Educational, Scientific and Cultural Organization, UNESCO, declared **Santo Domingo** Colonial City a World Heritage Site in 1990. Also popular are the resort communities on the east coast; **Punta Cana, Bavaro and Macao**. It is an all-inclusive resort heaven, with so many options; you will have a hard time deciding which resort to choose. On the north coast, the **Amber Coast**, **Puerto Plata** and the **Samana Peninsula** are also popular destinations. Carnival with all its fanfare will take you to another place in mind. It is celebrated during the month of February. Visit the website of the Dominican Republic Ministry of Tourism for more information.

Fun Facts

The Dominican Republic gets credit for creating the Merengue style of music, which is fast-paced, rhythmic dance music and moves.

The Amber Museum in Puerto Plata is known for having on display the amber stone with a prehistoric mosquito preserved inside, which was seen in the movie, *Jurassic Park.*

Baseball is the most popular sport in the Dominican Republic. U.S. professional baseball leagues sign scores of players to their teams who are of Dominican Republic descent.

Destination Dominican Republic

The Dominican Republic is a leader in environmental tourism and approximately 25 percent of the country's land and shores are preserved as national parks, reserves and sanctuaries.

Fashion designer, Oscar de la Renta, was born in the Dominican Republic.

Language
The official language is Spanish.

Currency
The Dominican peso (RD$) is the official currency. Most resorts do accept the U.S. Dollar.

Taxes
Hotels, restaurants and resorts charge 16% sales tax and 10% service charges.

Drinking Age
Drinking age in the Dominican Republic is 18.

Climate
The Dominican Republic has tropical weather year round.

Airports / Travel Documents Required
The Dominican Republic has eight international airports **including Las Americas International Airport (SDQ)** in Santo Domingo; **Punta Cana International Airport (PUJ)** and the **Gregorio Luperón International Airport (POP)** in Puerto Plata.

To travel to the Dominican Republic you will need to have a valid passport. Countries who have signed agreements, with the Dominican Republic, including the United States, will also need to purchase a Tourist Card. A Tourist Card is a US$10 tax on incoming tourists that can be purchased at the airport when you arrive. Citizens of other countries without a signed agreement will also need a Visa.

Upon re-entering the United States by air, all citizens, regardless of their age, must show a U.S. passport in book format.

For U.S. citizens, it is recommended that you sign up online with the Smart Traveler Enrollment Program (STEP). A Smart Traveler app is also available for

download for travel information. Visit the U.S. Department of State, Bureau of Consular Affairs website at http://travel.state.gov/ for additional travel advice and information.

Citizens of other countries should notify their country's embassy of their travel plans.

Disclaimer:

Documentation needed depends on your country of citizenship and residency. Although we do offer some information on documentation requirements, you will need to check the current entry requirements for your country of citizenship and not be dependent on the information presented here.

Punta Cana, Bavaro and Macao

The eastern coast of the Dominican Republic is home to lush tropical landscaping and luxury all-inclusive resorts. The area is also a golfer's paradise. The array of resorts are ready to help you plan your wedding to the smallest detail.

Local Attractions and Entertainment

Become a pirate for a night on **Ocean Adventures - Caribbean Buccaneers Dinner Show.** It is an interactive show that will take you back to the high seas of yesteryear. It is a must-experience.

Try your luck at the **Hard Rock Casino.** Casinos abound in the Dominican Republic. Many of the larger resorts and hotels operate casinos.

Walk the unbeaten paths of the **Indigenous Eyes Ecological Park.** Save on the cost by just paying the admission price and doing a self-guided tour. Be sure to take your swimsuit for a dip in the swimming holes.

Take a zip line tour of **Scape Park at Cap Cana** and sail above the tropical forests or dune buggy your way over the terrain.

Swim with the dolphins at **Manati Park** or visit with the iguanas, flamingos, tropical birds, snakes, crabs, or sea lions.

Puerta Plata, Playa Dorado and Samana Península

Puerto Plato on the north Amber Coast is home to many all-inclusive, budget friendly resorts, making it a good destination choice for fabulous destination weddings on a shoestring budget. An aerial tramway cable car system is located here and takes you for a journey up to the mountaintop. A replica of Christ the Redeemer statue, Rio de Janeiro, sits on top of one of its mountains. Elegant Victorian architecture can be found in the city. And of course, The Amber Museum is located here.

Local Attractions and Entertainment

Experience 27 waterfalls at the **Damajaqua Cascades.** No need to book ahead, especially if you are in a small group. Just grab a taxi for a 25 minute ride and pay the admission fee. It is your choice. You can canoe, hike, or splash in the waters!

At **Ocean World Adventure Park, Marina and Casino** you can experience a little of this or a little of that. After swimming with the dolphins, you can try your hand at the casino, or sit back and watch a show with sea lions entertaining you.

A must experience for anyone visiting Puerto Plata is taking a tram ride up the mountain with **Teleferico**! This is possibly a once-in-a lifetime experience.

Take a trip to **Paradise Island** for a day of paradise! Snorkel alongside beautifully colored marine life, or frolic on the beach. Or consider a ride on a speed boat over the turquoise blue Caribbean waves.

Visit the **Samana Península** for a true tropical one-of-a-kind experience. It is a whale watchers' heaven from January through March.

Tainopark offers a historical perspective of life of the Taino natives. It is a must-experience and gives guests the opportunity to go back in time.

Lay back at **Cayo Levantado, also known as Bacardi Beach.** This is a stunning beach to just lay and be a bum.

Sailing, swimming the waterfalls, scuba diving or exploring caves can all be done on the Samana Peninsula. Several **tours and adventures** for an experience that fits your interests are available in Samana.

Santo Domingo

A **Santo Domingo City Tour** is a must-experience for anyone taking a trip to the Dominican Republic. If you are staying at one of the all-inclusive resorts in the Dominican Republic, be sure to take a tour of the historic capital city, Santo Domingo. It is the oldest city in the Americas. Its rich culture is evident on its street with ancient cathedrals and cobblestone streets alongside modern architecturally designed buildings. Be sure to visit some of the museums while there!

While researching destinations in the Dominican Republic, be sure to check out the other resort towns not included here. We just list a sampling above to get you started.

MARRIAGE LICENSE REQUIREMENTS

Getting married in the Dominican Republic does not require residency or a waiting period. Also, blood tests are not required.

FDW Tip: To ensure that you are meeting the marriage license requirements for your destination wedding; it is highly recommended by the FDW team that you select a hotel or resort that has a specialty in wedding planning. You can then utilize their expertise and guidance to getting a marriage license and having a legal ceremony. Larger resorts and hotels will take care of the details for obtaining a marriage license.

Disclaimer:

Although we offer general information for getting married in various destinations, you will need to research the requirements of your home country and selected destination for the current requirements, laws, and regulations. We provide information here on Civil Ceremonies only.

Documents Needed

- Proof of citizenship - original copy of birth certificate
- Passport
- Single Status Affidavit certifying that you are singe and eligible to marry

- Certified Documents supporting any change in name
- Parental written consent, if under 18.
- Proof of divorce (if applicable) - certified copy or original Certificate of Divorce
- Copy of Death Certificate for widow or widower (if applicable)
- All documents must be authenticated by the couples' nearest Dominican Consulate before they arrive in the country.

Note: Documents must be authenticated by your nearest Dominican Consulate before arriving. Their services will also include legally translating the documents into Spanish. The marriage certificate will also need to be legally translated into English, after the ceremony.

Additionally, Dominican law requires that notice of the intended marriage be published prior to the ceremony.

Residency Requirement
There is no residency requirement or waiting period.

Marriage License
Issued by the Government of the Dominican Republic.

Marriage License Fee
Check with the offices of your nearest Dominican Consulate.

FDW Tip: Consult with your wedding coordinator at your hotel or resort, in advance, on requirements for obtaining a marriage license. Most resorts and hotels will request that you send them the documents months prior and will take care of the application process.

Ceremony
During the ceremony, the official asks the parties and witnesses whether either of the parties has been married previously, to each other or to other people. The party who has been married previously must supply the date of that marriage and the name of the person who officiated. Ten months must have elapsed since the divorce of anyone previously married.

A Fairy Tale Affair

Witnesses

Two witnesses over the age of 18 are required, and they must have identification. The Marriage Officer can also serve as a witness.

Note: Much of the information provided in this section was gathered from the Tourism Board or Bureau for the location. Please see the Directory for a list of Tourism Boards and Bureaus.

Chapter 5   Destination Mexico

Why Mexico? Because it's the place you thought you knew. Yes, Mexico has margaritas and mariachis. But Mexico also has 3000 years of history, 174 natural protected areas, and next to the United States, has more spas than any other country. All of this and more makes Mexico a top tourist destination, having something for every type of traveler and budget. Additionally, Mexico ranks high in all-inclusive resort options available, also making it one of the top destinations for weddings.

Destination Highlights

Mexico is the home of 30 UNESCO (United Nations Educational, Scientific and Cultural Organization) World Heritage Sites and as such these sites maintain the status of having special cultural or physical significance for the world. Although not widely known, Mexico has more than a dozen five-diamond resorts. It is a land of extremes, with mountains and canyons in the center of the country, deserts to the north, and dense rain forests in the south and east. In Mexico, you can visit ancient ruins and pyramids, have dinner at one of Mexico's many 4-star restaurants, and later gaze under stars at one of the many beachfront resorts that line the coasts. Popular tourist and wedding destinations include **Los Cabos**; **Playa del Carmen (Mayan Riviera)**; **Cancun** and **Cozumel**.

Fun Facts

The official name of Mexico is the United Mexican States.

Few nations support as many plant and animal species as Mexico.

Mexico introduced chocolate to the world, even before the Swiss. Chocolate was a part of some of the religious events for both the Mayan and Aztecroyal Indians.

Bullfighting is the national sport of Mexico, although soccer (futbol) is more popular. Bullfighting takes place from November through April.

An underground river 95 miles long with caves and caverns flows below Mexico's Yucatan Peninsula.

Mexico City is the oldest city in North America. It is also one of the largest cities in the world.

Destination Mexico

Language

The official language is Spanish.

Currency

The Mexican peso (MXN$) is the official currency. Merchants are not allowed to change U.S. dollars for pesos. Travelers, with passports for verification, can exchange foreign currency at Currency Exchanges at International airports. Some banks may also exchange money; however, not all banks provide this service. The most convenient way to make an exchange is at an ATM machine. Conversion transaction fees will be assessed and is typically 1 – 3%. Using a credit card for purchases is also a convenient way to make purchases. Your bank statement will show the exchange rate applicable.

Taxes

Mexico has a tax refund program and if you make purchases, spend at least 200 Mexican pesos at a business affiliated with the tax refund program, your purchases could be eligible. There are no tax refunds on services such as lodging and meals. To request your refund, on the day you leave the country, visit one of the tax refund kiosks located at certain airports nationwide. You will need to submit a completed form, your bank details, and other information. For more information on the tax refund program visit taxback.com.mx and www.taxfree.com.mx.

Drinking Age

Drinking age in Mexico is 18.

Climate

The climate in Mexico varies by region and time of year, so it is advisable to check the region that you will be traveling to for the average weather conditions and forecasts for the time that you plan to visit. Most people assume that it is always warm in Mexico; however, that is not the case. On the coasts the climate is generally balmy year-round, but some months are rainy, while others are dry.

Airports / Travel Documents Required

Mexico has over 50 International airports. For the cities and regions we highlight, the most popular International airports include: **Los Cabos International Airport (SJD), Cancún International Airport (CUN)**, and **Cozumel International Airport (CZM)**. Travelers to the Mayan Riviera book flights through the **Cancun International Airport**.

A Fairy Tale Affair

A valid passport is required to enter Mexico. A tourist card is also required and can be purchased at the airport. Major airlines will provide the form while en route to Mexico.

Upon re-entering the United States by air, all citizens, regardless of their age, must show a U.S. passport in book format.

For U.S. citizens, it is recommended that you sign up online with the Smart Traveler Enrollment Program (STEP). A Smart Traveler app is also available for download for travel information. Visit the U.S. Department of State, Bureau of Consular Affairs website at http://travel.state.gov/ for additional travel advice and information.

Disclaimer:

Documentation needed depends on your country of citizenship and residency. Although we do offer some information on documentation requirements, you will need to check the current entry requirements for your country of citizenship and not be dependent on the information presented here.

Los Cabos

Los Cabos encompasses the towns of Cabo San Lucas and San José del Cabo, as well as the Resort Corridor that lies between the two. The towns are also a popular cruise ship destination.

Local Attractions and Entertainment

El Arco de Cabo San Lucas (Lands End) is a must-experience of anyone visiting Cabo. The Arch is a natural geological rock formation and landmark and can be viewed from some of the resorts, but also by glass-bottom boat, water taxi, and tours.

Whale watching is a must-experience if you are visiting Cabo during whale watching season. **Whale Watch Cabo** offers tours that not only give you the opportunity to observe, but also appreciate and understand these mammals.

For the opportunity to swim with the Dolphins or take in a show visit **Cabo Dolphins.**

Located in the Chileno Bay, **Chileno Beach** is known for its coral reefs and attracts many snorkelers. **Playa del Amor (Lover's Beach)** is also a top-rated beach and very popular with couples.

Marina Cabo San Lucas Cabo is popular for its now upscale marina, shops, restaurants, and yacht watching. **Pedregal de Cabo San Lucas** is a popular spot to view million-dollar mansions on cobble-like stone roads.

If you feel like high speed real racing fun go to **Cabo Karting Center** for an adrenaline rush.

Mayan Riviera/Playa del Carmen

The Mayan Rivera offers impressive structures and sacred temples honouring Gods of the Mayan civilization. Playa del Carmen is located within the Mayan Riviera and is a popular stop for cruise ships. The Playa del Carmen community and government are committed to retain Playa del Carmen's reputation and charm as a small fishing village and artists' colony.

Local Attractions and Entertainment

A must-experience is a tour of a Mayan village through one of the many tour operators, including **Coba Mayan Village** and **Mayan Ruins of Tulum**.

To experience an underground water paradise, **Cenotes Sac Actun** is a must. Take a snorkeling tour to awe over underground caverns and caves and rock formations creating natural sculptures.

Learn about the local wildlife of the Yucatan at **Tulum Monkey Sanctuary,** a 60-acre ranch with rescued spider monkeys that live in a natural habitat.

For an adventure-themed amusement park, check out all the attractions and activities at **Parque Explor**. Zip-line, drive amphibious vehicles, or go river rafting. These are some of the attractions available at Parque Explor.

Enjoy the restaurants and bars and go shopping along **La Quinta Avenida**.

Cancun

Cancun was just a small sand barrier some 35 years ago. Today, Cancun consists of a medium-sized coastal city and a long, thin island connected to the mainland through bridges. You'll find a little bit of everything in Cancun, and a lot of other things. Cancun has strong clubs and fierce bar scene.

Local Attractions and Entertainment

Experience life of yesteryear as you take a dinner cruise on **Captain Hook Barco Pirata Pirate Ship**.

Learn about Mayan history at the **Museo Maya de Cancun**. Also consider visiting the ruins at **El Rey Ruins**. For a unique museum experience, stop by **Museo Sensorial del Tequila** for a tasting if you are visiting **Liverpool Mall**.

Interact or observe dolphins at **Dolphinaris Cancun**, **Interactive Aquarium** or **Dolphin Discovery**.

For shopping, browsing, breakfast or lunch, stroll down **Avenida Kukulkan** in the center of some of the beaches in Cancun. **Plaza Isla is** an outdoor shopping mall located on the lagoon side of Kulkulkan Blvd.

Of course, the stunning beaches are the main attraction in Cancun. Visit **Playa Delfines**, **Forum Beach Cancun**, **Playa Chac Mool**, or one of the other fabulous beaches or nearby islands.

Cozumel

Cozumel is a top diving destination and is known for its coral reefs and variety of natural beaches.

Local Attractions and Entertainment

For diving enthusiasts there are so many diving locations. **Santa Rosa Wall**, **Palancar Reef**, **We B Divin' Cozumel**, **Columbia Reef**, and **Diver Down Cozumel** are just some of your options.

Experience Mexican culture and tequila tasting at **Discover Mexico Cozumel Park**.

For an adventure theme park experience put **Chakanaab Park** on your to-do list. Here you can swim with dolphins, catch a sea lion show, zip line or snorkel.

A must-experience in Cozumel is the **Cozumel Bar Hop** tour. As you bar hop your tour guide gives you a tidbit of information about the area.

While researching destinations in Mexico, you may want to check out other cities and towns not included here.

MARRIAGE LICENSE REQUIREMENTS

Marriage license requirements are simplified by the wedding coordinator and staff at larger hotels and resorts. They will assist you to ensure that you have the necessary documents and follow the required procedures to get married legally in their country.

FDW Tip: To ensure that you are meeting the marriage license requirements for your destination wedding; it is highly recommended by the FDW team that you select a hotel or resort that has a specialty in wedding planning. You can then utilize their expertise and guidance to getting a marriage license and having a legal ceremony.

Disclaimer:

Although we offer general information for getting married in various destinations, you will need to research the requirements of your home country and selected destination for the current requirements, laws, and regulations. We provide information here on Civil Ceremonies only.

Documents Needed

- Passport
- Birth Certificates (Original and Apostilled copies translated into Spanish by authorized translator)
- Tourist Card or Visa. The names on the Passport and Tourist Card must be the same.
- Single Status Affidavit
- Civil Ceremony Form

- Proof of divorce (if applicable) - certified copy or original Certificate of Divorce. If the bride is divorced, a year must pass before she can re-marry. Also, if the bride is divorced and her passport is under her ex-husband's last name, then she must present her Birth Certificate and Divorce Certificate translated into Spanish by an Official Translator and should have an Apostille Seal.
- Copy of Death Certificate for widow or widower (if applicable)
- Health Certificate. After arriving to Mexico, couples are required to have a blood test taken and have chest x-rays performed to apply for a marriage license. Tests can be taken at most resorts and results are ready within 24 hours. Many resorts include the fees in their wedding packages.
- If the bride or groom are adopted, adoption papers are required

Legal Documents are not returned.

Foreigners marrying in Mexico must legalize their marriage in their country of birth/residence. In most cases this is done by registering your marriage certificate at your local City Hall, after your return.

The United States Department of State requires that all Weddings Certificates from ceremonies performed in the Caribbean, including Mexico, have the Apostille Seal.

Residency Requirement
There is a two to three-day waiting period to get married in Mexico depending on the state in Mexico you get married in. **Allow 3 business days for processing your marriage license application.**

Marriage License/Fees
Health certificate and administrative fees are estimated at $500.

> **FDW Tip: You will need to consult with your wedding coordinator at your hotel or resort, in advance, on requirements for obtaining a marriage license. Most resorts and hotels will request that you send them the documents months prior and will assist you in the application process.**

Ceremony
A Civil Ceremony is the only one that will be recognized as legal once you return to your home country. Since it is an official event, it is conducted in Spanish by a Judge and translated to English by a Wedding Coordinator.

Check to see if weddings are performed on Sundays. As of this writing, they are not performed on Sundays.

<u>Witnesses</u>
Four witnesses over the age of 18 are required, and they must have a passport and Tourist Card. Witnesses must arrive three business days prior to the legal wedding ceremony date in order to complete the legal document process.

Note: Much of the information provided in this section was gathered from the Tourism Board or Bureau for the location. Please see the Directory for a list of Tourism Boards and Bureaus.

Chapter 6   Destination Bahamas

Why the Bahamas? The Bahamas consists of more than 700 islands, conveniently starting just 50 miles off the Florida coast. Bahamas has the clearest water in the world with visibility of 200 feet down and the world's third largest barrier reef! It's easy to "Say Yes to the Bahamas" for your Destination Wedding!

Destination Highlights

The Bahamas lay claim to developed islands and untouched paradises. Academy Award winning actor, Sir Sidney Poitier, grew up on Cat Island. The **Exuma Cays** is a playground for the rich and famous, with numerous private homes, luxury resorts and beachside condos. **Nassau**, the capital of The Bahamas is a hub of Bahamian culture, shopping and nightlife. Blackbeard and his notorious band of pirates seized and settled in Nassau and terrorized the seas from 1716 through 1718. Blackbeard would first determine a ship's nationality and then have his crew raise that country's flag to not alarm the crew of the unsuspecting ship. The pirates would then raise Blackbeard's flag at the last moment. Popular tourist and wedding destinations in The Bahamas include **Nassau/Paradise Island**, New Providence and **Freeport, Grand Bahamas**. However, The Bahamas has many other island options, and you will want to do further research into them.

Fun Facts

Dean's Blue Hole on Long Island, Bahamas is the deepest blue hole in the world and is right next to the shore. You can go from knee deep water to a sudden drop off of 663 ft. Divers go to Dean's Blue Hole to attempt world records.

The Bahamas is the third richest country in the Western Hemisphere with the third highest GDP per capita.

Although The Bahamas has more than 700 islands, only an estimated 20 - 40 are considered to be populated. So in The Bahamas you actually could escape to a deserted island.

On January 17, 1977, it actually snowed in Freeport, although the snow did not stick, snowflakes were seen.

The song, *Who Let the Dogs Out?*, was sung by the Bahamian group, the Baha Men.

Language
The official language is English.

Currency
The Bahamian Dollar (B$) is the official currency. The U.S. Dollar is accepted because of the 1:1 exchange ratio.

Taxes
The Bahamas charge a Service Fee or Resort Fee to every person staying overnight. Hotels collect the fee of $18 per night per person as well as a $6 per person one time bellhop fee. This is in addition to the rate of the room and is not optional. There is no sales tax in The Bahamas.

Drinking Age
Drinking age in the Bahamas is 18.

Climate
The temperature is warm and pleasant throughout the year due to the Trade winds that blow almost continuously. The average temperature is in the 70s. Hurricane season officially lasts from June to November. It can rain year round, so there is no rainy season although it is heaviest in May and June. Thundershowers pass through quickly, so it generally does not ruin your day's activities.

Airports / Travel Documents Required
The Grand Bahama International Airport (FPO) serves travelers to the Grand Bahama Island, and **Lynden Pindling International Airport (NAS)** serves customers traveling to Nassau and Paradise Island.

Look for the Bahamahost decal on taxicabs and buses to experience knowledgeable, professional Bahamian hospitality as you travel in The Bahamas. Managed by the National Bahamahost Association, the program promotes professionalism, pride and education in hospitality fields to ensure a proper welcome to visitors.

Disclaimer:

Documentation needed depends on your country of citizenship and residency. Although we do offer some information on documentation requirements, you will need to check the current entry requirements for your country of citizenship and not be dependent on the information presented here.

For United States citizens, a valid passport showing proof of citizenship and photo identification will grant you entry to The Bahamas and re-entry to the United States. Upon arriving, everyone must fill out and sign an immigration form, keeping a portion of the card in hand until departing. U.S. citizens do not need a Visa provided that their stay is less than eight months. Canadian citizens may stay for three months without a Visa. Citizens of other nations will need to check with the Bahamian Embassy well in advance of travel. VISA requirements and maximum length of stay vary widely between countries.

Upon re-entering the United States by air, all citizens, regardless of their age, must show a U.S. passport in book format.

For U.S. citizens, it is recommended that you sign up online with the Smart Traveler Enrollment Program (STEP). A Smart Traveler app is also available for download for travel information. Visit the U.S. Department of State, Bureau of Consular Affairs website at http://travel.state.gov/ for additional travel advice and information.

Citizens of other countries should notify their country's embassy of their travel plans.

Nassau/Paradise Island

Nassau is the capital of The Bahamas. Paradise Island is minutes north of Nassau. 70% of the entire population of The Bahamas lives on Nassau. On Nassau and Paradise Island you can participate in award-winning attractions, shop for duty-free items to take back home, or stop and sip a Bahama Mama.

Local Attractions and Entertainment

Cable Beach is considered the hotel district of Nassau. Five enormous hotels are located on this strip. The area is also known for its dining, the Crystal Palace Casino, and the golden sand of Cable Beach.

To experience the world's largest marine park, visit **Marine Habitat at Atlantis** on Paradise Island. It is home to over 50,000 species of marine life.

Aquaventure Water Park at Atlantis Paradise Island is a 141-acre waterpark with water thrill rides Atlantean-themed towers, high-speed water slides, a mile-long

river ride with rolling rapids and wave surges, and 20 swimming areas connected by a lush, tropical environment.

Take a catamaran cruise across Nassau Harbour to **Blue Lagoon Island** and swim with the dolphins at this award-winning facility.

Visit the premier arts institute in The Bahamas, **The National Art Gallery of The Bahamas,** and view Bahamian Art and Visual culture.

Versailles Gardens and French Cloister are awe-inspiring manicured gardens set next to a 12th century Augustine monastery.

Freeport, Grand Bahamas

Freeport is located just 65 miles off the coast of Palm Beach, Florida. This has positioned it for tremendous growth for International business. Freeport has one of the world's largest underwater cave systems and three national parks.

Local Attractions and Entertainment

Kayak to **Peterson Cay National Park** to visit the smallest national park in the Bahamas at 1.5 Acre and spend the afternoon snorkeling for a spectacular underwater view of this tiny uninhabited island surrounded by beautiful coral reefs. It is only accessible by boat.

Lucayan National Park is a must-experience for a stroll through one of the most stunning beaches anywhere. Be sure to pack your swimsuit.

Visit the entertainment district of Freeport by taking a trip to **Port Lucaya Marketplace** and stop by **Count Basie Square** to listen to live bands on weekends.

For bird watching, tour the **Rand Memorial Nature Center** with a 100-acre wildlife reserve featuring many tropical birds.

MARRIAGE LICENSE REQUIREMENTS

Marriage license requirements are simplified by the wedding coordinator and staff at larger hotels and resorts. They will assist you to ensure that you have the necessary documents and follow the required procedures to get married legally in their country.

> **FDW Tip:** To ensure that you are meeting the marriage license requirements for your destination wedding; it is highly recommended by the FDW team that you select a hotel or resort that has a specialty in wedding planning. You can then utilize their expertise and guidance to getting a marriage license and having a legal ceremony.

Disclaimer:

Although we offer general information for getting married in various destinations, you will need to research the requirements of your home country and selected destination for the current requirements, laws, and regulations. We provide information here on Civil Ceremonies only.

Documents Needed

- Valid Passport
- Original or certified copy of Birth Certificate
- Single Status Affidavit certifying this fact must be sworn before a notary public or other person authorized to administer oaths in The Bahamas and declaration must accompany the application for a marriage license.
- Proof of divorce (if applicable) - certified copy or original Certificate of Divorce.
- Original or certified copy of Death Certificate for widow or widower (if applicable)

Foreigners marrying in the Bahamas must legalize their marriage in their country of birth/residence. In most cases this is done by registering your marriage certificate at your local City Hall.

The United States Department of State requires that all Weddings Certificates from ceremonies performed in the Caribbean, including The Bahamas, have the Apostille Seal.

Residency Requirement

The couple must be in The Bahamas at the time of application for a marriage license and must have resided in The Bahamas for at least one day prior to the date of their application. The couple must also produce evidence of the date of their arrival in The Bahamas. The Bahamas Immigration Card or entry stamp on your passport will suffice.

It takes two business days to process your application for a marriage license, excluding Bahamian holidays. An exception is made for passengers of cruise ships.

Marriage License/Fees

The fee for a marriage license is $120. Marriage licenses and certificates are issued by the Office of the Registrar General in Nassau. Office hours are Monday through Friday, 9:30 a.m. – 4:00 p.m.

Address: P.O. Box N-532 Nassau, The Bahamas

Phone: (242) 323-0594, (242) 323-0595, (242) 323-0597

Fax: (242) 322-5553

Couples wishing to be married on islands outside of New Providence and Grand Bahama Island can obtain a Marriage License at the Administrator's Office on that island.

FDW Tip: You will need to consult with your wedding coordinator at your hotel or resort, in advance, on current requirements for obtaining a marriage license. Most resorts and hotels will request that you send them the documents months prior and will assist you in the application process.

Ceremony

Weddings must be performed between sunrise and sunset. You can get married on the weekend, provided you make application during the work week. Also, there are several stores offering complete wedding rental attire.

Witnesses

Two witnesses, who are at least 18 years old, must sign your marriage license.

For additional information on getting married in Bahamas check with the wedding coordinator at your hotel or resort.

Note: Much of the information provided in this section was gathered from the Tourism Board or Bureau for the location. Please see the Directory for a list of Tourism Boards and Bureaus.

Chapter 7   Destination Saint Lucia

Why Saint Lucia? It's simply beautiful! Saint Lucia is a volcanic island with, the Pitons, forming the island's famous landmark and UNESCO World Heritage site. With its breathtaking views, gorgeous landscape, majestic beachfronts, and unspoiled rainforests, Saint Lucia has become a destination wedding choice for many couples, and offers all-inclusive resort options.

Destination Highlights

Saint Lucia is a lush Caribbean island and is what most people think of when they think of an island paradise. It is one of the Windward Islands and part of the chain of islands called the Lesser Antilles. With its dramatic twin peaks, the Pitons, soaring 2000 feet above sea level, its rainforest of wild orchids, giant ferns, and birds of paradise it is truly a nature-lover's dream vacation. Saint Lucia can also boast having the world's only drive-through volcanic crater, Saint Lucia's Soufriere volcano. You won't have to worry about an eruption during your visit; the volcano is dormant. Visitors and locals can be seen bathing in the mud from the mine springs close to the volcano for a natural spa experience.

Fun Facts

Each May, Saint Lucia hosts the Internationally-renowned Saint Lucia Jazz Festival. It has brought "cool" entertainment to locals and visitors for over 20 years.

Native only to Saint Lucia, the national bird is the Saint Lucia Parrot, or Jacquot.

Castries, the island's capital, has been destroyed by fires going back centuries; which is one of the reasons it is a modern city today.

Saint Lucia is over 50 million years old, with volcanic eruptions and earthquakes shaping its landscape.

As with many islands with a long history, it is believed that early inhabitants of Saint Lucia were cannibals, taking no (male) prisoners from their battle victories.

Language

The official language is English; however Saint Lucian Creole is spoken by most people.

Destination Saint Lucia

Currency

The East Caribbean dollar (EC$) is the official currency of Saint Lucia. Although the U.S. dollar is accepted, the exchange rate, which fluctuates, is currently US$1 to EC$2.65. Most hotels will make exchanges of foreign currency.

Taxes

There is a Departure Tax of EC$54 for all visitors leaving the island. There is a government tax of 8% on hotel and restaurant bills, in addition to a service charge of 10%. Be sure to check your bill before you pay, because they may have been already added.

Drinking Age

Drinking age in Saint Lucia is 18.

Climate

St. Lucia's temperature ranges from 65-85 degrees from December to May and 75-95 degrees from June to November.

Attire

Cool, comfortable clothing. Bring your favorite summer dresses and outfits; however, *beachwear is rarely appreciated off the beach.*

Airports / Travel Documents Required

St. Lucia has two airports: **Hewanorra International Airport at Vieux Fort (UVF)**; and **George F. L. Charles Airport (SLU)** which is near the capital of Castries.

Disclaimer:

Documentation needed depends on your country of citizenship and residency. Although we do offer some information on documentation requirements, you will need to check the current entry requirements for your country of citizenship and not be dependent on the information presented here.

Valid passports are required. Visas are not required for citizens of the U.S. or Commonwealth countries, or where there is an agreement for exemption between the home country and Saint Lucia.

Upon re-entering the United States by air, all citizens, regardless of their age, must show a U.S. passport in book format.

For U.S. citizens, it is recommended that you sign up online with the Smart Traveler Enrollment Program (STEP). A Smart Traveler app is also available for download for travel information. Visit the U.S. Department of State, Bureau of Consular Affairs website at http://travel.state.gov/ for additional travel advice and information.

Citizens of other countries should notify their country's embassy of their travel plans.

Local Attractions and Entertainment

While in Saint Lucia be sure to take a catamaran or water taxi to view **The Pitons**. It is a must-do for all visiting Saint Lucia.

Take a hike through **Pigeon Island National Park o**r take a dune buggy through the **Saint Lucia Rain Forest** to get up close and personal with Saint Lucia's flora and fauna.

Morne Coubaril Estate is the latest adventure park in Saint Lucia. It also offers a nice walking tour of the estate and you can zipline for an aerial view of the Pitons. It is a working mill and you can observe key steps in the making of sugar cane syrup, producing cocoa and coffee and processing coconuts for food products.

Enjoy a tasty burger at **Anse Mamin** a great little beach off the beaten path.

There are several horse riding stables on the island including **Island Riders**, **Holiday Riding Stables** and **Atlantic Shores Riding Stables**.

If you haven't driven an ATV, this is a must-do in Saint Lucia. With **Aanansi ATV Tours** you can take a trip through lush and mountainous banana, coconut and citrus plantations.

MARRIAGE LICENSE REQUIREMENTS

Marriage license requirements are simplified by the wedding coordinator and staff at larger hotels and resorts. They will assist you to ensure that you have the necessary documents and follow the required procedures to get married legally in their country.

Destination Saint Lucia

Disclaimer:

Although we offer general information for getting married in various destinations, you will need to research the requirements of your home country and selected destination for the current requirements, laws, and regulations. We provide information here on Civil Ceremonies only.

Documents Needed

- Valid Passport
- Original or certified copy of Birth Certificate
- Proof of Absolute, if one of the parties is divorced. Proof of divorce (if applicable) certified copy or original Certificate of Divorce.
- Original or certified copy of Death Certificate for widow or widower (if applicable)
- A Deed Poll if there has been a name change.

The United States Department of State requires that all Weddings Certificates from ceremonies performed in the Caribbean, including Saint Lucia, have the Apostille Seal.

Residency Requirement

Application must be made by a local solicitor to the Attorney General. There is a two-day residency requirement before a couple can make application for a marriage license. It takes an additional two "business" days to process the application.

Marriage License/Fees

Notarial Fees & Marriage License - EC$540.00.

Registrar Fees - EC$100.00

Marriage Certificate - EC$8.00

Note: It is possible to be married on the fifth day after arriving in St. Lucia, if the above procedures are followed.

> **FDW Tip:** You will need to consult with your wedding coordinator at your hotel or resort, in advance, on current requirements for obtaining a marriage license. Most resorts and hotels will request that you send them the documents required months prior and will assist you in the application process.

Ceremony

Weddings must take place between sunrise and sunset and cannot take place on holidays or weekends.

Witnesses

Two witnesses, who are at least 18 years old, must sign your marriage license.

For additional information on getting married in Saint Lucia check with the wedding coordinator at your hotel or resort.

Note: Much of the information provided in this section was gathered from the Tourism Board or Bureau for the location. Please see the Directory for a list of Tourism Boards and Bureaus.

Chapter 8   Destination Costa Rica

Why Costa Rica? In Costa Rica, you can experience the more than 130 species of freshwater fish, 160 species of amphibians, 208 species of mammals, 220 species of reptiles, 850 species of birds, and 1,000 species of butterflies. Or frolic through the 1,200 varieties of orchids or 9,000 species of plants because more than 25% of Costa Rica's land is dedicated to national parks, reserves and wildlife refuges with more than 100 different protected areas. It is also home to several all-inclusive resorts and is a popular destination wedding locale for couples to Go Costa Rica!

Destination Highlights

The Gulf of Papagayo is considered Costa Rica's posh spot located in the northwestern Guanacaste Province. Manuel Antonio, another tourist destination, has rolling jungle hills that surround Manuel Antonio National Park. It's also one of the most wildlife-rich regions in the world. In Costa Rica you can dine at great restaurants, dance the night away, take in a trip to an art gallery or take an adventure tour. Tamarindo, a surfer's heaven, is known for eco-tourism. Costa Rica is one of the most eco-conscious countries in the world. The Costa Rican Tourism Board awards Certification for Sustainable Tourism to differentiate between businesses in the tourism industry, based on the degree to which they comply with a sustainable model of natural, cultural and social resource management.

Fun Facts

Ever think about having home delivery of a Whopper or Big Mac? In Costa Rica, these fast-food chains deliver.

Milk, eggs and other like products are sold unrefrigerated, off-the shelf.

Women, when they marry, do not take their husband's last name. Women keep their full name for life.

There are no street addresses in Costa Rica and few, if any, street signs. You must know your landmarks to navigate around town.

Marine turtles have inhabited the Earth for more than 100 million years, surviving even the Ice Age, and Costa Rica has some of the most important nesting beaches for theses mammals.

Destination Costa Rica

Canopy Tours, or ziplining, originated in Costa Rica in the 1970's.

Language
The official language is Spanish, with English being the second language.

Currency
The Costa Rican Colon (CRC) is the official currency of Costa Rica. U.S. dollars are widely accepted, but be sure to check the exchange rate.

Taxes
There is a Departure Tax of US$29.00 of for all visitors, which can be paid in US Dollars, Colons or with a credit card. Sales tax is 13%. Other travel related taxes are 17%.

Drinking Age
Drinking age in Costa Rica is 18.

Climate
Costa Rica's climate is tropical overall, with two seasons. Dry season runs from January through May; while rainy season runs from May to November, December. The warmest months are March through May.

Attire
Pack cool, comfortable clothing. If you plan a trip into the jungle, also pack long sleeves and pants to protect yourself from insect bites. Take along trail shoes and socks for hikes.

Airports / Travel Documents Required
Costa Rica has four International airports. **Juan Santamaria International Airport (SJO)** in the capital city of San Jose and **Liberia's Daniel Oduber Quirós International Airport (LIR)** is the country's most northern airport.

Disclaimer:

Documentation needed depends on your country of citizenship and residency. Although we do offer some information on documentation requirements, you will need to check the current entry requirements for your country of citizenship and not be dependent on the information presented here.

A Fairy Tale Affair

A valid passport is required, as well as proof that you will be exiting the country before your passport or visa expires, usually within 90 days.

All travelers must also have either a return ticket or a ticket showing they will be exiting the country, referred to as an outbound, exit or onward ticket.

Upon re-entering the United States by air, all citizens, regardless of their age, must show a U.S. passport in book format.

For U.S. citizens, it is recommended that you sign up online with the Smart Traveler Enrollment Program (STEP). A Smart Traveler app is also available for download for travel information. Visit the U.S. Department of State, Bureau of Consular Affairs website at http://travel.state.gov/ for additional travel advice and information.

Citizens of other countries should notify their country's embassy of their travel plans.

Local Attractions and Entertainment

Costa Rica has an abundance of adventure tours. You have many options and several tour operators offering tours. A must-experience while in Costa Rica is to visit one of its beautiful National Parks.

The **Tombolo de la Ballena** is a great destination to observe Humpback Whales. Whales migrating from North America can be observed from December to April; while whales from South America, can be observed from July to October.

Go Adventures in Tamarindo offer tours with a variety of adventures from ziplining to horseback riding. Or consider rock climbing, white water rafting or a safari boat tour. If you are in the mood for bird or monkey or even crocodile watching, consider one of these tours.

For unique water adventures, **Sea Life Papagayo Tours** has several options including snorkeling, jet ski, and surfing tours.

Easy Tours and Transfers has many adventure tour options and offers ATV Safari tours, zipline tours, sport fishing among other options.

Destination Costa Rica
MARRIAGE LICENSE REQUIREMENTS

Marriage license requirements are simplified by the wedding coordinator and staff at larger hotels and resorts. They will assist you to ensure that you have the necessary documents and follow the required procedures to get married legally in their country.

Disclaimer:

Although we offer general information for getting married in various destinations, you will need to research the requirements of your home country and selected destination for the current requirements, laws, and regulations. We provide information here on Civil Ceremonies only.

Documents Needed

- Valid Passport
- Certificate of marital status
- If divorced, you need to send the date, place, name of court that decreed the divorce, and full name of ex-spouse, so that it can be included it in the sworn statement.
- If the bride has been divorced from previous marriage during the previous 10 months from the wedding date, certifications issued by two official Costa Rican Physicians stating that she is not currently pregnant.
- Original or certified copy of Death Certificate for widow or widower (if applicable)
- A Wedding Information Questionnaire must be completed prior to the ceremony.

Getting married in Costa Rica requires very little paperwork. There are no residency requirements, and no required documents other than your valid passport. You will complete a questionnaire that includes necessary data, and your Costa Rican lawyer will submit this as a sworn statement.

Residency Requirement
There is no residency requirement to get married in Costa Rica.

Marriage License/Fees
Check with your Costa Rican lawyer or Officiant for fees.

> **FDW Tip:** You will need to consult with your wedding coordinator at your hotel or resort, in advance, on current requirements for obtaining a marriage license. Most resorts and hotels will request that you send them the documents required months prior and will assist you in the application process.

Ceremony

In Costa Rica, only priests, judges and lawyers are legally authorized to perform a marriage ceremony.

Witnesses

Two witnesses are required to attest that they know the couple and that the bride and groom are each entering marriage by their own will and are each legally able to be married. The witnesses cannot be family.

Note: Much of the information provided in this section was gathered from the Tourism Board or Bureau for the location. Please see the Directory for a list of Tourism Boards and Bureaus.

Chapter 9   Destination Las Vegas and Cruise Ships

Why Vegas? Vegas is Wild with Style! In Vegas you have glitz and glam; world class entertainment and 5-star restaurants! If your taste says Paris, but your wallet says, "think again" then Vegas may fit the bill. Vegas has themed hotels to suit every taste. In Vegas you can ride a venetian-styled gondola, or take a trip up a replica of the Eiffel Tower. If you want a bit of the outdoors, Red Rock Canyon is less than a half hour's drive from the Las Vegas strip. Vegas is the original destination wedding location and hosts more weddings than any other place in the world!

Destination Highlights

In Vegas you have a host of options for your wedding. **Chapel of the Flowers** is a beautiful stand-alone chapel, and offers full-service wedding packages for all budgets. **Scenic Las Vegas Weddings Chapel** offers wedding packages that include ceremonies at beautiful scenic locations at points of interest in the Las Vegas Valley for a very unique wedding. **A Storybook Wedding Chapel** also offers full-service wedding packages and you can have Elvis show up to serenade you. **Vegas Weddings** offers full-service packages and the opportunity to have a casino-themed ceremony or Mediterranean-styled chapel amongst many other options. And of course the most famous, **A Little White Chapel** is still around after all these years and continues to offer full-service wedding packages. They also offer a drive-through wedding ceremony, literally. Where else but Vegas?

Fun Facts

An estimated 40 million people visit Las Vegas each year.

Seventeen of the 20 biggest hotels in the U.S. are in Las Vegas.

The Vegas area is home to the largest community of Hawaiians outside of Hawaii.

The famous Las Vegas strip is for the most part, not within the city limits of Las Vegas.

Many of the first hotels on The Strip opened in the 1950's such as The Desert Inn, The Sands, The Riviera, The Dunes, Hacienda, Tropicana, Royal Nevada, Moulin Rouge and The Stardust.

Destination Las Vegas and Cruise Ships

People would pour into Las Vegas to see The Rat Pack: Frank Sinatra, Dean Martin, Sammy Davis, Jr., Joey Bishop, Peter Lawford perform in the 1960's.

Language
The official language is English.

Currency
The U.S. Dollar is the official currency of Las Vegas.

Taxes
There is an 8.1% sales tax on purchases and a 12% tax on hotel rooms. Properties near Fremont Street Experience in Downtown Las Vegas incur a 13% tax on hotel rooms.

Drinking Age
Drinking age in Las Vegas is 21.

Climate
Expect hot summers in Vegas, while the winter months can be much cooler. Las Vegas's coldest month is December when the average temperature overnight is 36.6°F. In July, the warmest month, the average daytime temperature rises to 104.1°F. Here is a listing of the average temperature in Vegas for each month. In February Vegas experiences the most rain, and June is the driest month.

Jan	36.8°F	57.1°F
Feb	41.4°F	63.0°F
Mar	47.0°F	69.5°F
Apr	53.9°F	78.1°F
May	62.9°F	87.8°F
Jun	72.3°F	98.9°F
Jul	78.2°F	104.1°F
Aug	76.7°F	101.8°F
Sept	68.8°F	93.8°F
Oct	56.5°F	80.8°F
Nov	44.0°F	66.0°F
Dec	36.6°F	57.3°F

A Fairy Tale Affair

Attire

Dress according to the weather and forecast. During the day shorts, jeans or khakis, blouses, sport shirts with collars, and in good taste t-shirts is the norm. Evening attire is much more formal, and since you're in Vegas, dress to impress! Bring out that little black dress or formal dinner jacket.

Airports / Travel Documents Required

McCarran International Airport (LAS) serves the Las Vegas Community and is just a short shuttle trip or cab ride from the Las Vegas strip.

Disclaimer:

Documentation needed depends on your country of citizenship and residency. Although we do offer some information on documentation requirements, you will need to check the current entry requirements for your country of citizenship and not be dependent on the information presented here.

For domestic travel, between states, U.S. citizens are required to present photo identification such as a current and valid passport, driver's license or state identification card.

Non-U.S. Citizens and air travelers entering the U.S. are required to show a valid passport that expires at least 6 months later than the scheduled end of their visit to the U.S. A tourist VISA is required depending on your country and residency of citizenship. For more information on entry requirements go to http://travel.state.gov.

Citizens of other countries should notify their country's embassy of their travel plans.

Local Attractions and Entertainment

Vegas has star studded shows, an ever-changing array of attractions, new hotels, spas and great restaurants. Be sure to also check out www.vegas.com and also www.lasvegas.com for the most current information. Also, be sure to stop by the registration desk to register for player membership at the various casinos for discounts and promotions.

For a romantic dinner with a 360° panoramic view of Las Vegas be sure to make reservations for the award-winning **Top of the World** restaurant at The

Stratosphere Casino, Hotel and Tower. You cannot experience this anywhere else in Vegas.

Cirque du Soleil has many show options that will entertain you with dancers, aerialists and stunts that will keep you mesmerized.

Planet Hollywood Resort and Casino is now showcasing **Brittney Spears** in her own show, combining old and new music. Also check out the **Miracle Mile Shops** at Planet Hollywood for shopping, dining, and entertainment in glamorous surroundings.

For an all-you-can-eat dining experience, you have many options including, the buffets at **Caesar's Palace**, the **Wynn**, the **Bellagio** and the **M Resort and Spa**.

And of course, the highlight of any trip to Vegas has to include a stroll along the **Las Vegas strip** in the evening. Be sure to check out all the outdoor shows and attractions, including the **Bellagio Fountains** and the **New York-New York Roller Coaster**. Get a schedule of the various shows on the strip and plan your stroll.

MARRIAGE LICENSE REQUIREMENTS

Marriage license requirements are simplified by the wedding coordinator and staff at larger hotels and resorts. They will assist you to ensure that you have the necessary documents and follow the required procedures to get married legally in their country, or even in your home country.

Although we offer general information for getting married in various destinations, you will need to research the requirements of your home country and selected destination for the current requirements, laws, and regulations. We provide information here on Civil Ceremonies only.

Documents Needed

- Requirements for U.S. citizens and non U.S. citizens are the same.
- To obtain you marriage license, both parties must appear in person before a Clerk at a Clark County Marriage Bureau location. A marriage license allows a couple to marry in the state. It is not proof of marriage.
- All U.S. citizens are required to provide their Social Security number on the Affidavit of Application for a Marriage License. You do not need to present your Social Security card.

- Valid Passport (non-U.S. citizens)
- Valid photo identification: driver's license, state identification card. Identification to prove your name and age is required.
- Original or certified copy of Death Certificate for widow or widower (if applicable)

It is suggested that non-U.S. citizens check with their local officials for special documents needed to ensure their marriage is recognized in their country.

Residency Requirement
There is no waiting period for getting married in Vegas.

Marriage License/Fees
Marriage license fee is $60.

> **FDW Tip: Holidays are extremely popular for weddings in Vegas, so unless you have a strong desire to get married during a holiday, avoid getting married on a holiday or holiday weekend.**

Ceremony
Your marriage ceremony may be performed at any wedding chapel, church; the Office of Civil Marriages or anywhere your marriage Officiant is willing to perform the marriage ceremony in the State of Nevada. The expiration date of the marriage license is listed in the upper left-hand corner of your marriage license. Nevada marriages are legal and recognized all over the world.

At many of the hotel and casino chapels, wedding packages include all the vendors and services needed for your wedding including a wedding coordinator.

If you want an unusual wedding, then Vegas is ready to accommodate your request better than anyplace else.

If your reception is relatively small, you have many less expensive options to host your reception, including your hotel suite.

Witnesses
Two witnesses are required to attest that they know the couple and that the bride and groom are each entering marriage by their own will and are each legally able to be married. The witnesses cannot be family.

Destination Las Vegas and Cruise Ships

For additional information on getting married in Vegas check with the Wedding Coordinator at your hotel or resort.

Cruise Ships

Another destination wedding option is having your wedding on a fabulous ship. Yes, as you cruise to a fabulous destination. Many options and wedding packages are available, and for a hassle-free wedding, having the ceremony while cruising is a great option. With many cruise lines you have the option to plan a shipboard or shoreside ceremony. Be sure to research the various ship lines and ports-of-call along with costs if you choose this option. Just like all-inclusive resorts, cruise lines have packages that include everything you will need to have a Fabulous Destination Wedding, but also offer the opportunity to visit several ports-of-call.

Note: Much of the information provided in this section was gathered from the Tourism Board or Bureau for the location. Please see the Directory for a list of Tourism Boards and Bureaus.

Chapter 10   Selecting a Date

Selecting a date is one of the key decisions that will determine the cost savings of your wedding. This is especially true of destination weddings, since travel costs are directly related to the time of year that you choose to travel to a specific destination.

In general, peak season for most of the destinations that we suggest is December through late April. You will definitely want to avoid traveling to warmer climates during the winter holiday season and also during spring break times. For best travel rates to our suggested destinations, consider the months of April (later in the month), May, June, September, October, November and early December for the best rates. Also many warm climate destinations increase their rates for the summer, usually mid-May through August.

<u>Weather Conditions</u>

Weather conditions are a consideration for both local and destination weddings. For a hometown or destination wedding be sure to do your research when selecting your wedding date!

> **FDW Tip: For the best rates and to avoid hurricane season, our team considers early May as the ideal time for a fabulous destination wedding on a shoestring budget. Not only will you have your pick of fabulous all-inclusive resorts at bargain rates, but you will also be able to avoid crowds and not have the worry of hurricane season.**

Of course, not everyone will be able to schedule their wedding for early May. As with everything else in life, it will be a tradeoff. Do your research so that you select the best resort at the best rate possible at the best time of year for you.

After determining the bride and groom's availability, consider the availability of key guests such as parents, close family and friends. You will need to ask them about their availability so that your date accommodates their schedules and availability. You will need to confirm an entire week that everyone is available, to allow for pre and post-wedding activities.

It's best to have a first and second choice week that everyone is available, or most are available. When you make your reservation and deposit to secure a specific date for your wedding, you may need to consider your second choice for a better rate, or if the resort is booked.

When selecting the actual wedding day most couples think of Saturday. However, when you have a destination wedding, you are less limited to day of the week, since people have arranged to be away. Selecting Thursday or Friday as your wedding day allows your guests time after the wedding day to have a mini-vacation on their own, or with the group.

FDW Tip: The FDW team considers Thursday as the most ideal day for a Fabulous Destination Wedding. Friday is the best choice if you strictly look at it from budgetary concerns.

For a Thursday ceremony, the couple would arrive on Sunday or Monday (Earlier if required for a marriage license). The Wedding Party attendants and parents could arrive on Tuesday for wedding preparations and for attendant's "Night Out" party or bachelor/bachelorette party. Guests and family could arrive Wednesday, and as late as Thursday morning. If you are planning a late Thursday wedding, guests that arrive Thursday morning would still be able to make it to the ceremony, unless the airport is far. See chapter two on choosing a location. This helps guests who are on a budget and/or have time constraints.

The best reason for a Thursday wedding is that you get to relax and start your honeymoon earlier! For any event, you will continue preparing until the event occurs. By having your wedding on Thursday, you shorten your prep time and lengthen your honeymoon.

For most destination weddings, you do not need the extra prep time. Also, this will be an incentive for your guests to attend, since they will be able to squeeze in a mini-vacation.

Also, you will possibly be able to schedule this date with the resort, since most couples try to schedule a Friday or Saturday wedding.

The second best day to have your wedding, if Thursday doesn't work for you, would be Friday. You still benefit from some of what was mentioned above, but to a lesser extent. For a very small budget though, Friday is a better choice, because you and your guests could book your stay for fewer days. You could schedule everything a day later than stated above. You still benefit from having a weekday wedding and your guests could still have time to vacation afterward. For a mid-to-

large size wedding, it is recommended that you schedule Thursday or Friday for your wedding day. If the resort you are considering is booked, you will have to weigh advantages and disadvantages. Unless you have your heart set on only one resort, you may want to consider a different resort. The tradeoff for a different day may or may not be worth it for you. You will have to review your priorities.

One exception in favor of having a Saturday destination wedding (or any other day other than Thursday or Friday) would be if you can get a better rate, or you are planning a smaller wedding. Then you could extend your stay past the weekend into the next week because you would have fewer schedules to accommodate by having a smaller wedding. Otherwise, most guests will, generally, plan to return home on Sunday to be back at work Monday morning.

Once you have decided on your actual wedding day, the next decision will be to determine the exact date and time you prefer for the wedding ceremony. Do you want a sunrise wedding or sunset wedding? Or maybe you would like a mid-day or early evening ceremony. This will largely be dictated by availability at your resort.

FDW Tip: Early evening weddings are amazing because the sunset is a fabulous backdrop for the wedding ceremony and pictures. (See back cover)

Your resort will have time slots available for wedding ceremonies. Weddings that are scheduled for times between 4 PM and 7 PM benefit from being able to have a later reception. The wedding flows into the dinner hour, and the reception flows into a late-night party atmosphere.

Afternoon weddings are popular, and could accommodate extended picture taking sessions after the wedding. The reception could still be planned for late afternoon or early evening. Also, guests could get a jump start on their vacation.

Now, that you have your wedding week, day and time preferences, it's time to contact your selected resort and reserve it! Since the timing of your wedding is crucial to your having a Fabulous Destination Wedding, you will want to **lock in the date as soon as possible.** This is probably the most important activity you will need to do after deciding on the resort.

If you have opted for an alternative to an all-inclusive resort, you will still want to reserve and lock in your dates and times immediately. The best dates and times go quickly. For some resorts and venues, you will need to book your wedding a year

Selecting a Date

or more in advance. Otherwise, you may need to select your second or third choice wedding venue.

You will also want to know how flexible your resort/venue is if you need to make a change to your wedding date or time. Most venues will allow you to make a change if they have the date and time available.

Once you reserve your date and make your initial deposit at the resort, you can breathe a sigh of relief. The most stressful part of planning your Fabulous Destination Wedding is done!

Chapter 11   Select and Invite your Attendants

Who should you select and invite to be an attendant in your wedding party? Selecting your wedding party attendants is "not" just a matter of choosing your best friends and closest family members. This is especially true of destination weddings.

Some of your friends and family members that you would choose to serve as an attendant may not be able to attend for financial or other reasons. Also, since you are having a destination wedding, and people will be together for longer periods of time, it works best when people selected get along. Your mate's close friend that also is a wisecrack may not be a good choice, if s/he will make your other attendants uncomfortable over a period of time. Wisecracks that are fun in small doses can sometimes be annoying over a longer period of time. In destination weddings this is even more acute.

> **FDW Tip: The same attention given to selecting guests for a private dinner party should be applied when selecting guests for your wedding party. With a good mix of personalities, your wedding week could be a week long party culminating into the main event, your wedding! Their enthusiasm and excitement will spread to your wedding guests and everyone will have a great time. Everyone having a great time is one of the essentials of having a Fabulous Destination Wedding!**

A typical wedding has three to five bridesmaids with the same amount of groomsmen.

For larger destination weddings, this seems to hold true, as well, however there's no requirement to have three to five bridesmaids and groomsmen. For very small destination weddings, it is common to have just one bridesmaid and one groomsman. However, if you are planning a mid-to-large size destination wedding it helps to create a party vibe when you have at least three to five bridesmaids and three to five groomsmen.

The FDW team recommends a manageable amount of attendants even if you are having a large destination wedding. When you have more than 10 total attendants, more management is needed when communicating to the group, and keeping everyone on task.

Select and Invite your Attendants

The old tradition that there should be an equal amount of bridesmaids and groomsmen is no longer a requirement.

It is also important to select attendants that are reliable. In addition to selecting a good mix of individuals, having reliable attendants is crucial. With all the wedding details, it is important to surround yourself with reliable attendants. There's nothing worse than to have an attendant that is constantly late for events and activities. Avoid this by selecting reliable people at the beginning. This will make for smoother functions. Although one of your friends may be fun to hang around, if the person is not reliable then re-think making them an attendant. You may want to give them a more minor role in the wedding, instead.

Maid/Matron of Honor

Once you have your list of possible attendants, if you haven't already decided, you will need to select your Maid/Matron of Honor and Best Man. This may not be as easy a decision as you would think. The person you select should be "the" one person amongst everyone that truly supports you and whom you have shared many experiences over the years; and has been a part of your life recently. Especially for the Maid/Matron of Honor role, it is very important to select someone that you fully trust, in addition to being one of your closest friends or family members. If you have several friends vying to be your Maid/Matron of Honor, first of all, you are very lucky. However, select the person who you feel will do the best job, and politely tell the others that the person you selected has more time available at the moment to do everything that will be required for that role, or another polite excuse.

Best Man

The Best Man is usually the groom's closest friend. Since the Best Man has a very different role and gets far less involved in the details than the Maid/Matron of Honor in the wedding party, the selection of the Best Man, although important, is less crucial. The most important task of the Best Man is to toast the couple at the reception and a very close friend or family member will bring personal anecdotes to the toast.

Once you have decided on possible attendants, contact them as soon as possible, and ask if they will be able to serve in that role. It's best to ask in person, but if that is not an option, then a phone call is fine. However, do not send an email, text message or any other digital communication to request their participation, because how you ask them will set the tone for your wedding. At this point, you will also want to inform them that it is a destination wedding, inform them of possible

locations and the (probable) date of the event. You probably won't need more details than that at this time, but have information on the resort, estimated travel expenses, passport/ID requirements ready, and their duties, just in case.

Honorary Bridesmaids / Honorary Groomsmen

After contacting your list of possible attendants, if any will unable to travel to your wedding, they could be given the distinction of being an "Honorary Bridesmaid" or "Honorary Groomsmen" and listed in the program as such. That doesn't have to be decided now though. Also, some of your close family and friends will assist you and even possibly host pre-nuptial activities, but will not be able to attend your wedding. These individuals could also be considered for the honorary distinction and be listed in your program as such. Be sure to save a copy of your wedding program to give to these individuals when you return from your honeymoon.

The more involved your attendants are in the planning of your wedding activities and events, the more excited they will be the day of your wedding; so as much as possible get them involved early on. Below is a list of duties and responsibilities of the wedding party for a FDW. In local weddings, the list may include other items, however, for destination weddings the list below is the custom.

Attendants are expected to:

- Pay for their own wedding attire, shoes and accessories

- Pay for their own transportation and travel expenses. In destination weddings, although the wedding couple would like to take on this expense, if they had the budget; many do not, and it is no longer expected that the bride and groom pay for the travel arrangements for their attendants and guests.

- Attend prenuptial activities and events. Be on time. Hosting events for the couple is a nice gesture, but not a requirement, although many attendants do host the Bachelor/Bachelorette party or Bridal Shower.

- In destination weddings, it is not necessary for the wedding party to contribute toward a group gift because of the additional travel-related expenses

- Participate in wedding events and be on time

- Assist the wedding couple in other tasks, as needed
- Keep the enthusiasm going during the wedding week and especially at the reception

Maid/Matron of Honor:

- Holds the groom's wedding ring and the bride's bouquet during the ceremony

- Witnesses the signing of the marriage certificate

- Usually assists in the selection of the wedding party attire and accessories

- Usually coordinates or assists in coordinating the bridal shower

Best Man:

- If there is a Bachelor Party, the Best Man usually organizes it. For a FDW, we recommend that the Bachelor Party take place before departing for your destination.

- It is recommended that after the wedding party arrives to the wedding destination and a night before most of the guests arrive, that the wedding party have a "Night Out" event.

- Assures that the groomsmen and ushers are on time and properly attired

- Keeps the bride's wedding ring during the ceremony

- Witnesses the signing of the marriage certificate

- Toasts the bride and groom at the reception

- Dances with the bride, maid/matron of honor at the reception.

Bridesmaids (additional responsibilities):

- Supervise children in the wedding party, if asked

A Fairy Tale Affair

<u>Groomsmen and Ushers (additional responsibilities)</u>:

- Groomsmen usually also serve as ushers, escorting the Mothers of the Bride/Groom and grandmothers (and other guests, if needed) to their seats
- Lay aisle runner, if used
- Pass out wedding programs

Flower girls and ring bearers are not always a part of destination weddings. It is your choice if you would like to include them in your wedding. Children always spice up weddings because you never know what to expect from them, so the FDW team recommends including them, if possible. If you know children that are already coming, then they may be good candidates for these roles.

If you do decide to have a flower girl and/or a ring bearer, since the parents will also be attending and paying travel expenses, to keep down costs, you could give the parents the option of having the flower girl wear a white dress that they may already own, and the ring bearer could possibly also wear a coordinating ensemble that he already has in his wardrobe.

FDW Tip: The FDW team highly recommends getting as many guests personally involved in some aspect of your wedding, as possible, so that guests have an even stronger connection to your wedding and are vested in the success of the wedding and in everyone having a great time. Having one guest in a family actively involved, usually gets that person's whole family involved; so just one member per family would suffice.

Some roles that you could employ your guests to take on include serving as a hostess, usher, secondary photographer, participate in ceremony (i.e. recite a poem) or even serve as greeters at some events. If you have friends and family members that have unique talents find a use for their talent. You could also solicit their help prior to the wedding, maybe in assembling favors or some other task such as discreetly asking someone to watch a certain uncle at the reception who may drink a little too much.

Hostesses add a nice and needed touch to a medium-to-large size destination wedding. For a friend that may be close to the bride, or really wants to be a part of the event, but is not a bridesmaid, selecting the person(s) as a hostess is a nice gesture, and can really help out when you need an extra hand. The hostess can pass out wedding programs, pre-post ceremony appetizers or drinks or perform many other duties that may arise at the last minute.

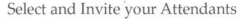

Select and Invite your Attendants

EXTRA: Some brides give special titles to their bridesmaids and include the title in the program. In addition to the "Maid of Honor" title, each bridesmaid could have their own unique title fitting their personality. A bridesmaid from New York could be called the "Maid of Manhattan" or "Lady of Long Island". However, if you give your bridesmaids titles of distinction, be sure that the person is aware of it, and that the title is a positive representation of the person. By using titles, all of your bridesmaids are distinguished, in addition to adding a bit of personality and whimsy, in keeping with *A Fairy Tale Affair*.

Chapter 12   First Things First – Legalities/Contracts

PASSPORTS

One thing, more than anything else, could ruin your plans for having a Fabulous Destination Wedding. That thing is your passport. Without this document your Destination Wedding outside the U.S. territories will not happen. More people than ever before now have a passport, however, many still do not or it will expire prior to completing their travel plans, or will no longer be valid for the trip. Some countries require passports to be valid for six months after your travel dates.

Remember, first things first. Do you have a passport and will it be valid through your return from your FDW? What about your close family members and friends that plan on attending and possibly even being a part of your wedding party. Do they have current and valid passports?

There have been many key guests that were unable to attend destination weddings because their passports did not come in time or were not valid, or would expire before the trip was completed. After you decide on having a destination wedding, immediately check the status of your passport and the passports of your family and close friends that you know will attend. You can check the Foreign Entry Requirements section of the U.S. Department of State website for the country you plan to have your Destination Wedding.

The FDW highly recommend that you and your guests, if applicable, apply for your passports at least 9 – 12 months prior to your trip. You will definitely want to know if you are going to have any hiccups or delays regarding your passports before you get deep into your wedding planning.

Visa

Some countries will also require a Visa, in addition to a Passport. A Visa is an endorsement on a passport indicating that the holder is allowed to enter or leave or stay for a specified period of time. A Visa is typically issued by an embassy or consulate. In some countries, Visas are issued to you upon arrival. Check with the U.S. Department of state for complete and up to date information on foreign country entry requirements.

Vaccinations

You will also want to check recommended or required vaccinations for your locale of choice. This information can be obtained at the website of the Center for Disease Control. Vaccines can take weeks before becoming effective or must be given in a series over a period of time.

Marriage Requirements

See prior chapters on general information and marriage requirements specific to the countries highlighted in this book. Many countries have residency requirements, such as 30 days, or 3 days. However, many popular destination wedding locations have 24 hour or no residency requirements. This will definitely impact your budget, so the FDW team highly recommends that you select a locale with the most lenient residency requirements. Considering a symbolic destination wedding is also an option for other locations.

Otherwise, you will have to pay for extra nights at the resort or hotel, prior to when you expected to arrive. You can obtain this information at the country's office of tourism. Again, the wedding coordinator at resorts and hotels are key resources on marriage license requirements for that locale.

You can also obtain this information at the U.S. State Department's website in the section, "Marriage of U.S. Citizens Abroad". Most countries will also require legal documents, such as birth certificates, or an affidavit of eligibility to marry. Again, check with that country's office of tourism.

Contracts

Prior to making your final selection on venues or vendors do a cost-comparison analysis of the different companies and resorts you are considering. Take into account what is included in each resort's wedding package. Because all-inclusive resorts have really cornered the market on destination weddings, many wedding packages will include the use of a Wedding Coordinator from the beginning of your wedding planning through your reception.

Be sure to save your electronic copies of all contracts and quotes. You will then have access to them when you arrive at your destination.

A Fairy Tale Affair

<u>Other costs that are sometimes included at all-inclusive resorts are</u>:

Officiant fees
Wedding ceremony site
Music
Decoration
Flowers (basic)
Wedding cake

You will want to compare these details to narrow down your resort selections. You will also want to do a cost-analysis of the resort with regard to room rates and amenities. After all, you want to select a destination with a variety of amenities that will appeal to you and your guests within your budgets. See Chapter 2 for additional information on choosing a location.

Once you have decided on one to three resorts to consider after doing your cost analysis, it is time to get actual quotes, to narrow down your search to your final choice. Your communication will, in most instances, be by email. You may contact the vendors and venue by phone initially, but often times, follow-up will be by email, because of time zone factors, convenience and costs. This actually is a benefit, because you receive everything in writing, and you will more than likely be in a different time zone. Be sure to save all of your written and email communications.

You will need to have an estimate number of guests that you plan to attend in order to get a more accurate quote. This is when the phrase, "The Devil is in the Details", really counts! Are all costs included? Are there extra charges for things that you did not anticipate? What is the cost of the reception, and what does that price include? Is liquor included in the cost of the reception? Are your selected upgrades included in this quote? What is the location back-up plan in case of bad weather? What form of payment does the locale accept?

You will need to review all costs by line item. You can always upgrade to a higher package or select an upgrade of an item, but be sure to get a "firm" quote before moving forward; and review any costs associated with any changes or upgrades you make.

Also, before you sign on the dotted line, you most definitely can negotiate the price. If the price does not appear fair, then ask for a price break or a lower price that fits your budget. A room upgrade for the couple is usually an easy upgrade to negotiate. Also up for negotiation are group discounts, especially if you are planning a medium-to-large FDW event with 50 or more guests. Headcount will have the most impact on your bottom line.

> **FDW Tip: The point of your negotiation is not to nickel and dime the company or vendor, but to get a fair price. After all, the companies do need to make a profit so that they can continue to host and provide destination wedding options for other couples.**

The most important consideration is to book and reserve your actual wedding date and time and wedding site on the resort premises. Be sure that this is clearly in the contract when you make your deposit and sign the contract.

Usually the initial contract that you sign will have changes that are made along the way. Many may be made after your arrival to your locale in meetings with your wedding coordinator. But avoid making any major last minute changes. Some couples have fallen for making major changes after smelling the sweet scent of the island flowers, and listening to the sound of the beat of the ocean. Remember, many minor details will not make a major impact on your wedding so unless it is something that you think really needs changing, avoid making major last-minute changes once you arrive.

Another advantage to booking your wedding at an all-inclusive resort is that you have a better handle on associated costs, so you are better able to control your budget. At the time of signing the contract with the resort, you will want to reserve blocks of rooms for your guests either through the resort or your travel agent. Of course, try to negotiate a group rate if you are planning a large wedding. Remember, you will be working with the wedding staff for several months, so you do want to develop a good relationship with them. Staff will go out-of-their way for customers and patrons that they like.

Travel Agent
To get the best rate on your accommodations, select one travel agent to book accommodations, and travel arrangements for yourself, and all of your guests. Reputable Internet travel agencies are fine. Sometimes it is more convenient, and cost-effective to work with a reputable online agency. Most travel is now done online, and most of your guests will call your selected agent to book their travel, so you don't need to go to a brick and mortar agency. Most communication with your travel agent will be done by telephone with follow-up by email, anyway. Guests could choose to book their airline travel separately to take advantage of reward

programs, though. It also may be a good idea to book any airport shuttle transfers through the travel agent.

FDW Tip: Have your guests set an alert on airline travel websites for notification of low rates so that they can book their airline tickets when they receive notification of a good rate. Kayak.com is a good resource for setting alerts for flights and plane tickets.

Your guests will be able to make payment arrangements through the travel agency, if needed. Once you have selected your travel agency/agent, create a spreadsheet for you and your agent to keep track of your guests that have paid, and who may need a nudge to stay on track with their payment schedule. This is a sensitive matter and therefore, guests need to be treated with extra consideration, courtesy and confidentiality.

FDW Tip: The FDW team highly recommends that a payment schedule or calendar be included on your website to serve as a reminder for your guests to make payments toward their hotel/resort accommodations through the travel agent. You can also include other dates such as suggested deadline date to apply for passport, and possibly other pre-wedding activities. This is crucial for large wedding parties. Also track your guests' travel itinerary on the spreadsheet so you know the day and time when your guests will arrive at the resort.

Chapter 13   Guest List

A typical destination wedding could include 25 - 40 guests. When deciding the size of your FDW, first, decide if you want a small, wedding with just close friends, or a larger affair. If you prefer a smaller event, then typically this will include your closest family and friends. Generally, the larger your family, then the larger your guest list. Here's a guide created by the FDW team to help you in your decision making:

Fabulous Destination Wedding – Wedding Guest Guide

Elope (2) – Couple only / Solicit witnesses on site
Private (3 – 8 guests) – Closest family and friends, one bridesmaid, one groomsman
Intimate (8 – 12) – Close family and friends and attendants
Close Friends and Family Affair (12 – 25) – Family, close friends, and attendants
Friends and Family Affair (25 – 75) – Family, friends and attendants
Friends and Family Major Affair (75+) – Family, distant relatives, friends,
        associates, and attendants

To get started, the bride and groom need to compile separate lists of their family and friends. There will probably be some overlapping of friends. After compiling separate lists, look the lists over and be sure to include others that weren't on either list. Since your guests will be paying their own traveling and hotel/resort expenses, your final list will be much smaller, so you can safely over invite. To ensure that many of your family and friends are able to make your wedding, give them as much notice as you can, preferably 9 – 12 months in advance. Also, let them know what is required to travel to your destination wedding locale. Review chapter 12 on working with a travel agent and creating a guest list spreadsheet.

When making your deposit for your wedding for the resort, keep your number of guests conservative; your list will pare down once it is time for your guests to make their initial hotel/resort deposit, or payment. Many of your friends will say they are coming, until it is time to make payment. You can always add people to your wedding party list for the resort, as needed. Even after making their deposit and making payment to attend, a few guests, at the last minute, may not be able to attend after all.

You will want to give your guests as much notice as possible so that they can make travel preparations, including possibly applying for a passport or submitting a request for time off of work. The fastest way to spread the news will be to utilize technology. Because you will be unable to invite all of your Facebook and Twitter friends, avoid using Facebook and other social networking sites. Phoning and following the phone call with an e-mail works best. By calling each invited guest personally, you set the stage for your wedding by extending courtesies and special treatment to each of your guests.

After you have compiled your guest list, immediately get contact information, including email and complete home addresses and cell phone numbers for your invited guests and identify those that are comfortable with technology, which will be most people. Some may still prefer snail mail or phone calls, possibly older guests.

Even if you haven't created your wedding website yet (See Chapter 14), contact all of your guests, personally invite them and let them know your preliminary wedding plans, including date, locale and resort. Also let them know travel requirements, such as passports. That way your guests have a heads up if they need to apply for a passport. Anticipate the procrastinators, and have frequent communication with them.

FDW Tip: More of your guests will attend, if you make each of your guests feel special at the very beginning with your initial contact to them. By initially calling or speaking with them personally, you set a positive tone for your wedding. Also, be sure to make the process of attending as affordable, convenient and as hassle-free for them, as possible.

It is not necessary to send *Save the Date* postcards. Email and e-communication is much more efficient and cost effective. Also in keeping with curbing your expenses, consider foregoing with formal invitations. For destination weddings, they are not necessary and you have a host of e-communication options. After calling your guests and sending them a follow-up email or e-communication, keep your guests updated through your wedding website and email/e-communication.

Create a group email distribution list to send updates to each of your guests. Each time you update your wedding website, send a quick email to your guests to let them know and include a link to your wedding website with additional information. Guests that do not have email you will need to call to let them know any updates.

FDW Tip: The key to having a Fabulous Destination Wedding on a shoestring budget is to avoid purchasing items that will have little or no-impact on your special day. Spend your money on items that will have the most impact.

Each of your guests will have to go way out of their way to attend your destination wedding, in addition to incurring a large expense, so take this into consideration when making your plans. Most importantly, if you want to have a Fabulous Destination Wedding, avoid turning into Bridezilla!

Chapter 14   Creating Your Wedding Website

Wedding websites are ideal for Destination Weddings and you can personalize it specific to your wedding details and information for guests. Websites serve so many purposes that it is a must for any couple planning a Fabulous Destination Wedding. There's an abundance of complimentary websites that couples can use to host their FDW details.

When reviewing websites the following considerations should be taken into consideration:

1. Security and privacy of site
2. Price – Free or complimentary
3. Features and options
4. User-friendly
5, Limited advertisements

Some of our favorite websites for hosting personalized wedding websites include the following: Wedding Window, Wedding Wire, and Offbeat Bride. Be sure to take the necessary time to apply creativity and personalization to your site. In essence, you want your wedding website to be the beginning of creating the mood for your wedding!

> **FDW Tip:** Everybody loves a great love story, and your website is the place to tell YOUR story. It gets people excited about both of you as a couple and the desire to see you in wedded bliss. Every couple has "their" song. Be sure to include yours on your website, along with pictures of the both of you.

Here's a list of recommended items to consider for your wedding website:
1. Your Love Story
2. Your Song - *Playing in the background*
3. Gallery of pictures - *Couple pictures and baby pictures*
4. Your wedding and location details. Update this section as details are finalized.
5. Travel resource information for guests:
   - Travel agent contact information
   - Passport and Travel information
   - Cellphone and ATM usage information for your destination

6.   Gift registry information. Although you will definitely not be requesting gifts, and your guests' attendance is gift enough, the gift registry is for those individuals that will be unable to attend.

Also, some guests that plan to attend will also want to purchase a gift. You might be surprised, but you will probably get gifts from several of your guests that attend your destination wedding. In addition, business colleagues, family and close friends will most likely purchase a gift. Guests prefer a gift registry, so that they are purchasing something that the couple wants or needs.

7.   Guest comment section for guests to your website to publish comments or messages of congratulations. The best websites are interactive and get participation from users and guests that go to the website.

> **FDW Tip: Use audio and visual effects. It will make your website exciting and engaging and keep guests returning to it, to check for updates.**

8.   Include information about your destination locale and hype up the location. Become an ambassador for your destination wedding country.

9.   Regularly update your website to keep it interesting. Initially, you will not have many updates, but as you finalize plans, you will. However, only notify guests with an email if it is a major update.

Note: Avoid sending an email at a time when someone else in your family or circle has a major event. Be sensitive to others' special events.

Whenever you communicate with family and friends regarding your planned wedding details, be humble and gracious in all of your communications both oral and in writing. Above all else, follow proper etiquette protocol when designing and communicating through your website.

Chapter 15   Creating Your Wedding Program and Name Cards

It's time to get creative! With all the software that is on the market today, you have the perfect opportunity to create programs that are works of art. Well, maybe not quite; however, your programs can be engaging to read, along with being informative.

First, decide the order of the ceremony. This very crucial step sometimes gets overlooked. Couples sometimes get so inundated with the glitz and glamour of creating a Fabulous Destination Wedding that the basics sometimes get left out. First, decide the events and special moments you and your mate want to include in your ceremony. Find what speaks to your personalities, culture, and the love you have for one another. One of the FDW team's favorite destination friendly activity is the pouring of the unity sand. See Chapter 20 for additional ceremony suggestions.

Pouring the Unity Sand
You and your mate each have different color sand and you pour the sand however you want, into one clear vase or vessel. Be sure to fill the jar to the rim and place a lid on the top, if you want to preserve the pattern when traveling. This is a fun, meaningful activity that represents your blended and undivided love…a perfect choice if you are getting married on the beach! (See back cover)

Next, you will need to decide the order of events and activities and who is participating in those activities or events. Again, you will want to reference Chapter 20.

FDW Tip: The FDW team recommends that the couple envision their ideal ceremony from start to finish at the onset of planning their wedding. For a Fabulous Destination Wedding we encourage that you create a storyboard to help you visualize every detail. Beyond the basic details, take into consideration the creation of "feel good" memories for yourself and your guests. Many special moments will just happen if the stage is set. So, set the stage. With that said…by having a destination wedding, half your job of setting the stage for special moments to occur, is already done!

Decide the order of the reception

When planning the order of events and activities at the reception, allow for more wiggle room and flexibility within the schedule. Plan your events with approximate times. It is more important that you or the host/DJ gauge when your guests are ready for the next event and let that override the schedule. For example, don't rush your guests to the dance floor when they are enjoying great food and conversation. See Chapter 21 for additional reception ideas.

Creating the Programs

When creating the look of your programs, you may want to incorporate the theme and colors of your wedding. You can have a formal wedding program with beautiful paper stock and fancy fonts or something that specifically relates to the destination. You can choose to create a formal program or a crossword puzzle for your guests to complete. It's a destination wedding, not a traditional affair, after all; you have the creative license to be wacky and wonky, if you choose. Your programs will become nice keepsakes for your guests, so have fun creating them and take your time. When it's all over, you and your guests will love having every memento from your Fabulous Destination Wedding.

> **FDW Tip: Pinterest.com is a great resource to help spark your own design creativity.**

Wedding/Reception programs are very easy to create and there are several online templates to assist you with your vision. Just buy paper and ink, and then, create! You can even buy patterned stamps, stencil, or cut outs to add more design and texture to your programs. If you aren't the DIY type, then you may want to consider one of the several discount stationery online sites to have them create your programs. Typically, there are fewer destination wedding guests than guests for a local wedding at home, so you will save by requiring fewer items, because of the smaller headcount.

Printed Menu

When creating the reception programs it is thoughtful to include the menu, especially if you choose to serve buffet style and the food is exotic. Be sure to check with the hotel wedding coordinator or catering service about any special dietary requirements of your guests (i.e. diabetic, vegetarian, allergies, etc.) Don't let your guests go hungry...It's no fun when your wedding guests can't enjoy the party due to their growling stomach and fatigue. The Menu can be printed separately, or on the back of the Reception program.

Seating Chart and Name Cards

Create your seating chart or diagram weeks before you arrive and discuss all the details with your coordinator. It will help your coordinator to place the name cards in each appropriate section. Keep in mind you don't have to use name cards, you have other options; however, if you want the formal-ness of name cards, go for it. The cost is minimal; it just takes time to create them. Again, "you either spend time of money".

If you decide to have assigned tables instead of seats create an easy viewable table list or decorate a fun way to direct your guests to their assigned tables.

> **FDW Tip: Round tables, 72", seats 10; and a 48" table, seats 6. Keep this in mind when making your seating chart.**

Places to Purchase Stationery, Supplies, and DIY Kits

You can purchase stationery supplies at Costco, Office Depot, Party City, your local arts & craft or stationery store.

Online Wedding Stationery Companies

Some online wedding stationery companies you may want to consider include: Wedding Paper Divas, Minted, Amazon, Etsy, eInvite, and VistaPrint.

Downloadable Computer Software to Create Stationery Designs

Illustrator, Photoshop, and Apple Pages are great options when designing your programs. Many online programs have a free 30-day trial period so design away and find what works best for you. If you find software that you like, consider purchasing for future use.

Chapter 16   Wedding Theme, Colors and Attire

A white dress with a long, flowing train and a veil that is even longer, or a simple knee-length white dress with the bridal bouquet being the primary adornment. Whatever your choice, saving money on the cost of your wedding attire is one of the best ways to trim your wedding expenses. With all the options currently available you can stay within budget and still be fashionable and fabulous!

Browsing magazines and online websites will assist you in developing the theme and colors for your wedding. Stay flexible, with regard to colors, because a fabulous bridesmaid dress may come in limited budget-friendly color options.

You will find lots of guidance on wedding attire for destination weddings. The team at FDW differs in that regard to an extent. Many bridal gown designers will have a collection dedicated to destination weddings. The typical destination wedding dresses are less formal and have fewer adornments.   After considering possible cultural and religious restrictions, if that applies to your wedding, wear what you like and what looks best on you and is appropriate for the climate/temperature. After all, you are having a Fabulous Destination Wedding, who needs to wear typical? If you want to wear a dress with a long train, go for it! Trains and long veils don't touch your body, so they won't generate heat.   A bride at a beach ceremony with a gorgeous floor-length gown with long train and flowing veil is stunning!   A bit of bling that sparkles in the bodice at sunset is breathtaking.

FDW Tip: The main considerations when selecting a wedding gown are:
1.   Cost
2.   Styles that compliment your shape and weather conditions
3.   "THE" Dress – one that you love!

Cost

For a Fabulous Destination Wedding on a shoestring budget, cost has to be the number one priority. Once you decide on a budget for your dress, you will be able to find styles and gowns that you love. Yes, really.   With that said, the FDW team also feels that if you do splurge anywhere for your wedding, then let it be on your gown.

> **FDW Tip: To have a Fabulous Destination Wedding, one critical ingredient is to feel fabulous…"When you look good, you feel good!"**

So feel free to splurge a little on your wedding gown, within reason. Many fabulous gowns have been purchased at thrift stores, white elephant sales, and on sale at retail stores. Others have been borrowed or passed down from family members. Also, formal white dresses are purchased as wedding gowns by many budget-conscious brides. Adding a label, "wedding gown" simply doubles or triples the price. And although this may be contrary to popular belief, designer gowns start at a budget-friendly $500, retail. Just be sure to allow 3 to 6 months for delivery of your gown and an additional 2 to 4 weeks for alterations.

Also, unless you are soliciting the help of a <u>professional</u> seamstress as a gift; the FDW team advises against having your dress made by yourself, friend or family member. Too many things could go wrong with having a dress made. Also, trying on dresses and looking for "THE" dress is part of the fun of getting married and is essential to having a Fabulous Destination Wedding.

Style
The style of your wedding dress is very important. The style and type of dress that you choose will say more about you and your personality than anything else. Who are you? Who do you want to be? Do you have cultural or religious considerations? Do you prefer classic styles or the latest fashion trends?

When selecting dresses to try on, you will find yourself gravitating to a certain style. That will be your comfort zone. So try on many different dresses and many different styles. Get out of your comfort zone! You may find a dress that you would have never considered if you had not tried it on. We all have experienced clothes that look plain on the hanger and fabulous when we try them on. It is no different with wedding dresses. So have fun, check out bridal gown magazines, browse online stores, and clip or save dresses that you like. This will make your gown shopping go much smoother when you actually are at the bridal salon selecting and trying on dresses.

A Fairy Tale Affair

When trying on gowns, the first order of business is to narrow down the silhouette. Wedding gowns come in many silhouettes:

A-line
Ball gown
Trumpet
Sheath
Mermaid
Empire Waist
Peplum

Certain silhouettes are recommended for certain figures and shapes. Your bridal gown consultant will be able to assess which silhouettes she feels would work best for you. However, do not limit yourself to these suggestions. Be sure to try on different silhouettes and styles to make your own assessment. The more you familiarize yourself with wedding gowns and silhouettes the better prepared you will be when selecting and trying on gowns. To make productive use of your time at the bridal salon, (and avoid much frustration), be sure to take the clippings of dresses you saw in bridal magazines and online with you. This will guide the consultant to select gowns that match your taste and style. Pinterest and other online bulletin boards are very useful applications to use to file pictures of dresses you like when browsing gowns online. However, you may want to limit access to your web page to keep your wedding plans a surprise to guests.

FDW Tip: Take or wear appropriate undergarments for several different silhouettes when trying on dresses. Also bring heels or shoes that will be the same height of the shoes you plan to wear.

Necklines and fabric are also to be considered when selecting a dress style, especially for destination weddings. Although the FDW team suggests that you wear a dress that you love, if you are in the beating sun with a high neck dress or a dress with long sleeves, you will begin loving that dress less and less as your wedding day progresses.

FDW Tip: When trying on wedding dresses, take a couple of close friends, wedding party attendants, or family members with you to the bridal salon. Avoid taking a big group to avoid confusion and frustration. Most importantly, leave your well-intentioned, highly-opinionated friends and family members at home.

"THE" Dress

You will know it when you try it on!

Groom / Male Attendants

The groom and his ushers have many choices when deciding on wedding apparel. They can choose to rent tuxedos, or even parts of a tuxedo, such as the pants and vest, without the jacket. For destinations weddings, because of the warm climate of the locations of many destination weddings, the men in the wedding party usually go a little more casual for comfort. The male attire can add just that bit of playfulness to remind guests that this is a destination wedding on a beautiful, tropical paradise. Be creative with the male attire. However, since you are planning a Fabulous Destination Wedding, be sure that the male attire complements the theme of your wedding.

A Fairy Tale Affair

Chapter 17   Wedding Day Prep and Packing

Careful packing and preparation is essential to having a Fabulous Destination Wedding.

FDW Tip: In preparation for the week of your Fabulous Destination Wedding, the FDW team recommends that you create at least four checklists: a Pre-departure Checklist; a Checklist or Schedule of Activities and Tasks to be done after your arrival to your destination; a Wedding Day Checklist, and a Vacation Checklist to include items to pack for your Honeymoon.

Pre-departure Checklist

A checklist of items and last minute tasks to complete before you leave for your destination is a must. Keep in mind that you are on vacation so don't forget about your other vacation needs and attire outside of the wedding. The list below represents many of the items you may want to include on your checklist:

FDW Tip: The FDW team suggests storing secure electronic file copies of your passports and IDs in case of emergency.

<u>Note</u>: VISA credit cards and debit cards are more widely accepted globally; and if you are planning to use it at an overseas ATM machine, many foreign ATM machines only accept 4-digit pin codes. If your pin code is longer than 4-digits, you may want to have it re-set before you depart.

Pre-Departure Checklist
Photo Identification / Driver's License
Passport
Travel Documents
Marriage License Documents
Debit / Credit Cards
Single dollar bills for tips at the airport and resort or hotel
Medication
      Prescription medicines
      Pain reliever/aspirin
      Antacid
      Allergy medicine
Laptop/PDA/Tablet/Smart Phone

Chargers for devices

Wedding Day Attire / Gown / Tuxedo **(Carry on - DO NOT CHECK at airport)**

Bible (If needed)

Other items

<u>Note</u>: Store electronic files of your vendor contracts, phone numbers and wedding details. Pack hard copies of contracts if you do not have them stored electronically, or if needed.

Schedule / Checklist -Tasks and Activities

A schedule of your activities for the wedding week should be created after meeting with your Resort/Hotel Wedding Coordinator after your arrival. Also reference other chapters regarding your schedule. Items on your list could include dates and times of the following:

Schedule Checklist – Tasks and Activities

Meet with Wedding Coordinator

Finalize wedding ceremony / reception details and schedule with Wedding Coordinator

Have gown pressed, if needed

Couples' Pre-wedding massage, if planned

Schedule appointment with stylist

Put together Welcome Letter / Gift Bag for guests

Meet with Officiant

Meet / Teleconference with DJ and/or entertainment

Wedding Day Checklist

Create a wedding day checklist of everything you will need the day of the wedding and also list the tasks that need to be completed. You will want to check this list before you depart for your destination to ensure that you pack everything needed. You also may need to update the list after you meet with your Wedding Coordinator. The night before your wedding, be sure everything is checked on the list that will be needed for the ceremony and reception. Items needed and tasks needing to be completed for the day of your Fabulous Destination Wedding could include:

Confirm final ceremony details with your Wedding Coordinator

Schedule / Timetable of Wedding Day activities

Wedding Ceremony Items

Reception Items

Gown/Tuxedo and all other wedding attire: shoes, veil/headpiece, jewelry, undergarments, accessories, etc.

Make-up, hair and beauty supplies, including pony tail holder for emergency up-do

Wedding Day Emergency Kit: chalk (to be used to cover up any spots that may get on your white gown) safety pins, bobby pins, needle and thread, feminine products, eye drops, extra pair of contact lenses, protein bars

Vacation / Honeymoon Checklist

Your vacation / honeymoon checklist will be the most fun list to create. Although you probably would not create a vacation checklist at other times, because you have a wedding and other pressing items, you won't want to forget something you will need for vacationing because you are so focused on your wedding. Items on this list could include the following:

Swimwear
Sunglasses
Sunblock
Vacation clothing and footwear
Camera
Phone Charger
Toiletries

Packing

Most importantly be sure to check that your gown will be ready for pick up at least 30 days prior to your wedding day to avoid any last minute emergencies. You can't pack a dress that still needs to be picked up!

Call your airline, in advance, for guidance on requirements to carry on your bridal gown to avoid any last minute surprises. Also, inform your bridal gown retailer that you plan to have a destination wedding and ask if they have any special garment bags, or wrapping or suggestions for your specific dress to help it keep its shape and prevent it from wrinkling while traveling. Otherwise, use tissue paper when packing it in its garment bag. If it does wrinkle, be sure to have it steam-pressed by your resort or hotel, immediately after arrival.

When you arrive at your destination unpack in an organized manner, so that you put things away in order of when you will need them for the week, keeping your wedding day items and other specific event or activity items grouped together.

Wedding Day Prep and Packing

To ensure that your Fabulous Destination Wedding is a *Fairy Tale Affair*, be sure to start checking off your lists!

Chapter 18   Wedding Week Activities

As the Bride or Groom of a Fabulous Destination Wedding, you also will serve as Activities Director for your guests. Since your guests will be traveling to attend your wedding, and because you will need them available for certain activities, it is best to do an itinerary of wedding activities and events. The FDW team recommends that you include the guest itinerary in their welcome package, which is discussed in Chapter 19.

When making the itinerary, it is best to pencil in the final details after your arrival after you meet with your Wedding Coordinator. You will need to be prepared to print copies of the itinerary for your guests, so be sure to speak with the resort personnel about computer and printing services in advance.

When setting your itinerary, the first order of business will be to start with the dates and times of the required events. Also, you may want (2) itineraries: one for your guests and one for your Wedding Party Attendants (bridesmaids, groomsmen). If you choose to just have one itinerary, be sure to be polite when referencing those activities that are for the Wedding Party Attendants only.

For example, for the wedding rehearsal, you may want to add a comment:

> "Wedding Rehearsal – Beachfront, 2 PM, Bridal Party Required (All other guests get to relax and enjoy the resort.")

Since the rehearsal dinner will be right after the rehearsal, there's no need to put that in the itinerary, unless you choose to combine the rehearsal with the Welcome Party for smaller weddings. Otherwise, if you just have one itinerary, the FDW team recommends that you do not broadcast the rehearsal dinner in your itinerary.

To keep the bridal party on track with all their events, and activities having (2) itineraries would be a good idea. The itineraries need to be decided and printed before the attendants arrive. After you meet with your Wedding Coordinator, later that evening, if not earlier, complete and print your itineraries. Do as much prep work in advance of leaving your hometown, so that you are only updating the information.

FDW Tip: It is highly suggested that all business matters and paperwork be handled prior to any of your guests or attendants' arrival. Things start getting really hectic after that, and time will be at a premium. Do not take for granted the time that you have when you first arrive. Use your first couple of days wisely. Upon arrival, tour and become familiar with the resort, so you can ask questions of your Wedding Coordinator, and can assist your guests, when needed. Then take care of business! You will have plenty of time to relax later.

You will need to plan and prepare for your wedding activities.

Suggested activities:

Wedding Party Attendants' Night Out
Welcome Reception / Meet and Greet
Group Breakfast
Wedding Rehearsal
Rehearsal Dinner
Wedding
Reception
After Party

Attendants' Night Out

Depending on the day of the week your wedding is scheduled, schedule your Attendants' Night Out event the night of their arrival. It is best to arrange for the attendants to arrive at least (2) days before the wedding. So if you are planning a Thursday wedding, arrange for the wedding party attendants to book their flights early on Tuesday to arrive Tuesday afternoon, and plan to go out that night and have fun! As discussed in prior chapters, it is best to avoid a Bachelor or Bachelorette or Bridal Shower party while at the destination. Those should be done before leaving your hometown.

Welcome Reception / Meet and Greet

The Welcome Party or Meet and Greet is generally scheduled the night that most your guests arrived. This may also be the same day as your Wedding Rehearsal and Rehearsal Dinner. It is best to schedule it after the dinner hour since you will probably be having it right after the rehearsal dinner. 7 PM – 9 PM would be a great time to schedule your Welcome Party if you have that flexibility. It could be something simple, such as all your guests meeting at a location on the resort, or you could schedule something more elaborate. Here is another advantage to having your FDW at an All-inclusive resort.

A Fairy Tale Affair

The resort may have a location that is less frequented during these hours, and you could possibly arrange to have your Welcome Party event at that location. Another option for a budget friendly Welcome Party, if your parents are attending and staying in a Suite, you could schedule to have your Welcome Party in their suite. Look for inexpensive ways to host your event. Some bars at hotels and resorts with private sitting areas could work just fine. Scout around for a good spot when you arrive, if you haven't already chosen the location of your Welcome Party.

As mentioned, try to schedule the Welcome Party / Meet and Greet immediately following the Rehearsal Dinner, later in the evening. The day's events could begin with the rehearsal from 2 – 3:30 PM, Rehearsal Dinner at 4:00 PM and the Welcome Reception / Meet and Greet following the Rehearsal dinner at 7:30 PM. It's a good idea to have this decided or at least have some options before arriving. The number of guests (headcount) that will be attending your wedding will narrow down your choices. Again, if you choose to have your wedding at an all-inclusive resort, then the drinks will probably be on the house at the hotel's bar!

Arrange for your parents or an adult member of the family or close friend to facilitate/host this event. It would have to be someone that you are very close to and can pull this off, to get everyone to participate. So only assign this to someone who knows most of the people in attendance, and would be comfortable speaking. If you do not have anyone that could do this properly, then the FDW team recommends that the Bride and Groom co-host the event, themselves. This event will set the tone for the rest of your wedding activities so it needs to get the proper attention. The Welcome Party should include:

- Welcome (Given by Bride and Groom or Parents of Bride and Groom)

- Introduce all of your Guests or do a Round Robin. A Round Robin for larger groups would entail soliciting one family member or member of a specific group to introduce everyone in their family or group present.

- Most importantly, you want everyone to feel special, so try to find something special to say about everyone in attendance. DO NOT MISS ANYONE! Think about this in advance. It may come naturally, but just give it a few thoughts in advance, just in case. Note: You (bride/groom or person hosting the reception) can then add a special comment about your relationship with that person or group after they are introduced.

- Review the itinerary, wedding time and location. Pass out additional copies of the Welcome Letter to anyone who may not have received it from the front desk. (See Chapter 19)

- Game/Ice Opener

Thank everyone again for coming – Ask if they have any questions about the wedding schedule or planned events for the week.

Group Breakfast

It is highly recommended by the FDW team that a group breakfast time and place be scheduled for every day leading up to, the day of, and the day after the wedding. This will help your guests get to know each other in a casual setting and forge bonds. Guests have the option to come early for breakfast if they want to chat a bit, or come a little later, if they want more private time. Just be sure not to make any hard-set rules; just make it an open invitation.

This is another advantage to having your wedding at an all-inclusive resort. Everyone can meet up for breakfast and the cost is already included. Nobody has to worry about how to split the check, or possibly not going, if they are on a tight budget. It is recommended that breakfast is scheduled between 7:30 and 8:30 AM. The early birds can come early, and still be around when the night owls come down for breakfast. Also, if anyone wants to avoid the group breakfast, they can come down earlier without offending anyone. It is not expected that everyone will attend the group breakfast.

FDW Tip: The breakfast the morning after the wedding is usually not attended by the Bride and Groom, however the FDW team highly suggests that the Bride and Groom make a "surprise" appearance at the Group Breakfast, the morning following their wedding. Consider this your last organized wedding event.

Because everyone will be a bit tired from the wedding festivities, it is recommended that it be scheduled for later in the morning, 8:30 or 9AM. Everyone will be overjoyed and surprised that the Bride and Groom chose to get up and have breakfast with the group, instead of sleeping in late. This will not be expected, and do not tell the guests that you will be joining them for breakfast. Come down a little late and surprise everyone. This will make it very special for the guests and a gesture of appreciation for them coming to your destination wedding.

A Fairy Tale Affair

After this final Group Breakfast, guests may choose to break off into their private groups for breakfast and other activities going forward, this will depend on the size of the group, the number of families attending and other factors. This would be fine; the guests will now be in vacation mode. If you were lucky enough to be able to schedule your wedding on a Thursday, then your guests will have plenty of time to explore, relax, or do whatever they prefer to do while on vacation, with most guests departing on Sunday. The guests will consider it a treat if they happen to run into the Bride and Groom, but, it is your time now….time for you to vacate and honeymoon knowing that you took very good care of your guests and had *A Fairy Tale Affair!*

Normally the Bride and Groom will arrive on Sunday or Monday, but this is totally dependent on the marriage license requirements. For some destinations, it is required that the couple be at that location 24 hours in advance of obtaining a marriage license, while other countries have no waiting period. Below is a sample itinerary for a Thursday wedding:

Suggested Sample itinerary for a FDW "Thursday" Wedding

Sunday	Bride and Groom arrive
Monday	Meet with Wedding Coordinator
Tuesday	Wedding Party Attendants and Parents arrive / Attendants' "Night Out"
Wednesday	Group Breakfast / Guests arrive / Wedding Rehearsal / Rehearsal Dinner Welcome Reception (Meet and Greet)
Thursday	Group Breakfast / Wedding / Reception / After-Party
Friday	Group Breakfast / Bride and Groom Honeymoon / Guests vacation
Saturday	Bride and Groom Honeymoon / Guests vacation
Sunday	Bride and Groom Honeymoon / Guests depart
Monday	Bride and Groom Honeymoon
Tuesday	Bride and Groom depart

Note: You will just need to add the times for your events, and adjust depending on the day that your wedding takes place.

If possible, schedule (2) weeks off from work for your Fabulous Destination Wedding or try to arrange working from home for part of the time. You then get to have time after you return to adjust to being married, unpack, and get situated before you get back to your normal routine. Most of your guests are going to schedule their flights to depart on Sunday, so you may want to take a couple of extra days after everyone has departed, to continue your honeymoon.

Many couples have confessed that they had more fun on their honeymoons because of their interaction with their guests and continuing to do activities as a group with their friends. This is especially true for close friends. However, we recommend that the couple spend some quality time alone, and if possible schedule some additional days after all of your guests have departed to Honeymoon alone.

Wedding Rehearsal

The resort's Wedding Coordinator that you will be assigned will coordinate the wedding rehearsal in most situations. Any details that you have or would like to have implemented should have already been discussed with your Wedding Coordinator. The best advice we can offer here is to listen to your resort Wedding Coordinator. She (or he) does this every day and knows what tends to work best. BE FLEXIBLE! However, if something doesn't seem quite right, mention it. They are open to doing things that you suggest. Most importantly, be sure that your attendants arrive on time, preferably early.

You will have a small window of time to rehearse. If you have your own personal coordinator (not necessary, but some couples assign a close friend or family member this duty) be sure to work with your Resort Coordinator. It is best if they follow the lead of the Resort Coordinator to avoid confusion. It is best to time the Wedding Rehearsal dinner right after the rehearsal. It forces your rehearsal to stay on schedule, and you avoid a scattering of the group, and delay in the rehearsal dinner, if it is planned immediately after the rehearsal.

Wedding

Enjoy! Today is your day. Trust that things will go well. Most importantly, again, people need to arrive on time. Be sure to gently emphasize that to your Attendants, in advance. It's best, and more fun, if the Bridesmaids and Bride get dressed together. After the Bridesmaids are dressed, they can assist the Bride. To ensure ushers are available for early guests, have the Groomsmen arrive to the wedding location early to serve as Ushers. This also ensures that the groomsmen are on time. Also, the Groom needs to ensure that his guys are on time. Once the guests arrive, it flows! (See Chapter 20)

Reception

Party! Your DJ or MC will be taking over from here. You should have met with him in advance with scheduling of activities, music and special requests. This is

A Fairy Tale Affair

another advantage of using the recommended DJ/MC suggested by the resort. The DJ will be used to the routine and the order of how receptions are typically handled at that resort. See Chapter 21 for more information regarding your Reception Party.

Eat, drink and be merry. Food, drinks and music in a faraway land…Dance the night away! You are living a real-life *Fairy Tale Affair.* Party up!

Chapter 19   Welcome Letter and Gift Bags

At destination weddings it is typical for the bride and groom to give their guests a gift and / or welcome letter. A gift is given as a token of appreciation for the guests having had to travel a long distance, and most importantly, paying the expense, to attend your wedding. A gift is a nice touch, but only if it fits in your budget. A well-drafted welcome letter on nice stationary would suffice, as well, if you do not have the budget for gift bags. You could roll the letter and tie it with a pretty ribbon! For an additional touch you could attach gourmet candy from the gift shop.

The Welcome Letter will be the key piece of communication with your guests when they arrive. In addition to creating excitement, and showing your appreciation to your guests; it should also inform the guests about the wedding week activities, dates, times, places, and key contact information.

Because plans may change after arrival, it is best to have a draft of the letter, and print it once you have gone over details with your resort-assigned Wedding Coordinator, prior to the arrival of your first guest. A well-drafted letter will be personal, create excitement and set the tone for your Fabulous Destination Wedding. Ultimately, it will get your guests ready and eager for all the wedding activities to come!

You should also include destination hot spots for down-time and post-wedding things-to-do, and places-to-go. Be sure to include, local "must-see" places and "must-do" activities, popular restaurants, and shopping venues. We included many hot spots and attractions in our destination chapters 3 – 9.

Also, most of this can be reviewed and researched in advance, before leaving home, and included in your welcome letter draft. Once your room is assigned and the time and places for events are finalized with your wedding coordinator, update your Welcome Letter, and print it after your arrival at the resort. Be sure to pack stationery and envelopes to bring with you.

<u>A well-formatted letter will be one page, front and back and include</u>:

Front Page: Welcome
Thank you/Welcome paragraph
Resort amenities (Select a few to mention)
Destination Venues and Hot Spots (Research in advance / See chapters 3 - 9)

Host/Hostess Room - Room #

> **FDW Tip:** Be sure to indicate on the front side that letter continues on back side.

Back Page: Itinerary
Pre-Wedding Events
 Meet and Greet/Welcome Reception
 Family Breakfast
Pre-wedding activities that you have planned
Main Event (Wedding)
Post-Wedding Activities
Contact information, and room number of key people such as bride, groom and parents. This information will not be known in advance, so that is another reason to have the final draft of the letter printed after your arrival.

> **FDW Tip:** Be sure to include the day, dates, times and locations that guests need to be present at events; so that there is no miscommunication of dates and times when the events and activities are scheduled. Be sure to include the day of the week, along with and the date and time.

> **FDW Tip:** It is already suggested by the FDW team that the bride and groom change rooms to an upgraded room or suite, if possible. It is not expected for the wedded couple to give that room number to guests.

The welcome gift or bag can be elaborate or simple. First, avoid a gift basket, because it is too bulky. Stick with a medium-sized decorative gift bag and ribbon, which can be purchased in advance, inexpensively and travels well. (Do not pack the bags in advance.) Since our focus is to have a FDW on a shoestring budget, we recommend that budget-friendly token gifts be purchased.

Although it is recommended by many wedding planners to purchase welcome gifts after you arrive at your destination, we at the FDW team recommend that you select simple items that travel well, and are not bulky or heavy, in advance. You will have enough things to do after your arrival and limited time to select gifts. Also, you may not be able to find budget-friendly gifts in the gift shop. It is typical to give one gift bag per room; a group gift bag. You should have already created a spreadsheet, at this time, with who will be sharing rooms.

A Fairy Tale Affair

It may take some research to find nice budget-friendly gifts and gift bags that travel well, so start searching well in advance. The Internet is a great option, and you may be able to find gifts themed for your destination locale.

FDW Tip: Try to do as much prep work in advance of traveling to your destination wedding locale to avoid last-minute stressors.

If you do wait until you arrive to purchase the welcome gifts, consider contacting the hotel/resort gift shop in advance for possible options and costs.

The Welcome Gift / bag should include the welcome letter, and token gifts. Avoid cluttering the gift bag with travel brochures. Your guests can pick them up for themselves from the lobby. If you do plan a group event, you may want to include a brochure for that place.

Possible gifts to include in the gift bag could include:

Candy (Could be as simple as hard candy purchased in bulk, wrapped in cellophane and tied with a bow)

Snacks

Beach towel

Flip Flops

Travel-size suntan lotion / bug spray / specialty toiletries

Luggage tags

Reusable tote bags

Postcards (purchased at gift shop) and nice colored-ink pens (purchased in advance)

Gourmet coffee / specialty teas (Be sure package travels well)

FDW Tip: A well-wrapped gift will make your guests feel that you put extra effort into it and make them feel special, no matter the cost of the gift. So plan in advance, stick to your budget, and get creative!

Chapter 20   The Wedding Ceremony

The wedding ceremony is the main event of the week's festivities! If you have chosen to have a destination wedding, then you probably have also opted to remain flexible with the wedding ceremony. If you are highly religious and want to ensure that your ceremony reflects and follows your religion's customs, then you will have to do additional research about having a religious ceremony in your destination wedding locale beforehand. Some couples opt to have a separate religious ceremony in their hometown.

Most couples that choose to have a destination wedding will need to be flexible with regard to wedding details; although the same could be said of hometown weddings. Rarely does a wedding go exactly as planned.

Officiant

Most destination wedding venues, hotels, and resorts will have a dedicated Officiant that they use, or a list in which you could select an Officiant. Take in consideration the advice of your resort's Wedding Coordinator. They usually work with the same Officiant and vendors, and have already pre-screened their recommendations, or consistently work with them on weddings. Your wedding will go a lot smoother if you work with vendors and people that are accustomed to working together already. They have an established rhythm and method, and by their experience of working together, weddings can go more like clockwork; everybody already knows their job and what to expect.

In this instance, a destination wedding can be much smoother than a hometown wedding. It would be beneficial to know if the Officiant will be attending the wedding rehearsal. Typically, the Officiant at destination weddings meets with the couple early in the week, but does not always attend the rehearsal.

The resort's on-site Wedding Coordinator typically runs the rehearsal, along with any designated coordinator that the bride and groom may provide to assist.

On-site Wedding Coordinator

Your resort will have assigned you an On-site Wedding Coordinator that will be working with you on all details of your wedding events, including coordinating the wedding rehearsal. Trust in the suggestions of your On-site Wedding Coordinator. They do weddings every day and know what works best. However, be sure to discuss your ideas about your ceremony in advance of the rehearsal. Your coordinator should be sent a copy of your wedding program in advance of

your arrival, and at the latest, at one of the early meetings that you have upon your arrival, to iron out any details.

Ceremony

Most weddings follow a certain structure. This is especially true of destination weddings. When selecting the elements that you want included in your ceremony, and the people to participate in these activities, the FDW team highly suggests that you incorporate elements that reflect both families, the bride's and the groom's. The wedding should also be the coming together of families.

You may want to have an opening prayer by a member of the bride's family and the closing prayer by a member of the groom's family. Be sure to have a bible available, because this has been forgotten by many couples, and had to be fetched at the last minute. Inform the person that will say a prayer to please bring their bible. If you have two people saying prayer then hopefully, at least one will remember to bring it with them. Otherwise, you can get a bible from the hotel.

If one of your attendants or guests is also an accomplished singer or vocalist or musician, you may want to include them in the program to perform. However, many destination weddings do not have an entertainer on the program.

Components of the Ceremony

Although the wedding is the main event, many couples wait until the last minute to create their wedding program, especially for destination weddings. Because you will need to ask people in advance to perform or do readings or say a prayer, you should create your preliminary program several months in advance to give selected people who will be participating in your ceremony time to prepare. Also, you will want to print copies of your program at least 2 – 3 weeks before the event and will need the details finalized by then.

Standard ceremony components are included on the following list; however, most couples personalize their ceremony with elements important to them or that reflects their personality. One word of caution is to take into consideration that you will be making a statement as a couple, and ask yourself, "What do I want my wedding to say about me and us as a couple?" By having a destination wedding, your wedding already stands out, and is quite personal. Very offbeat wedding ceremonies, although very personal, could be considered inappropriate by local customs.

Sample Wedding Ceremony:

Processional Music
Processional

        Officiant
        Groom's grandparents
        Bride's grandparents
        Groom's parents
        Bride's mother
        Best Man (for FDW, Best Man can walk down the aisle)
        Groom (for FDW, Groom can walk down the aisle)
        Groomsmen and Bridesmaids
        Maid of Honor
        Ring bearer
        Flower girl
        Bride and Father of the Bride

Officiant's opening remarks
Prayer
Vows
Exchange of Rings
Other Unity customs
Reading or Poem / Performance / Song
Pronouncement
The Kiss
Recessional music
Recession

        Bride and Groom
        Flower Girl/Ring Bearer
        Maid of Honor / Best Man (Paired up for efficiency in exiting)
        Bridesmaids / Groomsmen (Paired up for efficiency in exiting)
        Guests
            First Row (Both sides)
            Second Row (Both sides)
            Etcetera
Receiving Line / Group Picture

FDW Tip: It is highly recommended by the FDW team that the entire wedding party and all guests line up for a group photo immediately after the ceremony. The recession would lead to the group photo location to take a group picture.

The planning of the group wedding picture will have to be planned in advance. It is best to make an announcement about the group picture, or mention it in the program so guests do not scatter.

The Wedding Coordinator and photographer will have to assist with lining everyone up. Make sure to inform both in advance, and also your guests so that this moves quickly. For many guests, the group picture is one of their most treasured mementos from the wedding!

Many couples, after the group picture and also after receiving and acknowledging their guests, will take wedding party and family pictures at this time. It is best that this goes as quickly as possible. Some couples offer champagne sips and a light cocktail hour during this time before the reception.

Program
The wedding program, in addition to stating the order of events, serves several purposes. An artistic and tastefully-designed program is also a keepsake for guests. It also allows the bride and groom the opportunity to acknowledge and show appreciation to individuals that helped make their wedding a very special event. *Be sure it is error-free!* (See Chapter 15)

A sample program format is offered below:

Cover Page
The format for typical wedding programs consists of 8 ½ X 11 card stock or stationery, folded in half like a book.

The cover page typically reads "The Matrimony of", and includes the names of the bride and groom at the top. A picture of the couple is usually placed in the center of the page or superimposed. The day, date, time and location of the matrimony are typically at the bottom.

Inside Left Page
Wedding Program / Order of Service
Note: Include full names and titles (i.e. Officiant) of the individuals that will have individual tasks in your ceremony. This allows you the opportunity to further recognize and acknowledge these individuals for their contribution.

A Fairy Tale Affair

<u>Inside Right Page</u>

Names of Wedding Party Attendants and Honorary Attendants

> Names of Parents of Groom
> Names of Parents of Bride
> Name of Maid Of Honor
> Name of Best Man
> Names of Bridesmaids
> Name of Flower girl
> Name of Ring Bearer
> Names of Honorary Attendants
> Names of Host/Hostesses
> Names of Ushers

<u>Back Page</u>

The back page should include a special thank you paragraph to your Wedding Coordinators and others who may have gone above and beyond. Be sure to include the name of the resort's Wedding Coordinator.

The next paragraph will include a thank you to each of your guests for attending, and have their names listed, individually. Paragraph format is fine, and avoids having your program look like a form. Guests will appreciate that you have included them with a thank you in your program; and everybody likes seeing their name in print. IT IS CRITICAL THAT EVERYONE'S NAME IS LISTED.

Have fun creating your program!

Chapter 21   The Reception and Honeymoon

You're married and it's time to party! The reception is a celebration of your marriage and the uniting of two families together as one. The FDW team suggests that you have a flexible timeline of your planned activities. Be sure to communicate all of your needs with your resort-assigned Wedding Coordinator and your DJ/host. It's your party you can do what you want.

Here's a list of reception activity ideas you might want to include:

- Newlywed Entrance -This is a fun way for the bridal party followed by the newlyweds to enter the reception. You could choose to enter the reception in royal fashion or dance your way in. This is your special entrance so have fun with it.

- Special Dance Duets -

     The First Dance. In true wedding fashion it's proper etiquette that no one is allowed to dance on the dance floor until the couple has had their first dance.

     Father and Bride or Mother and Groom Dance. You and your mate have two separate dance duets with one family member of your choosing,

- Family and Bridal Party Champagne Toasts

- Cake Cutting

- Garter and Bouquet Toss

- Dinner

- Party time

FDW Tip: Have two separate playlists for the DJ. One playlist is for specific songs you want played during special activities in the program, for example, a meaningful song picked especially for the First Dance. The other playlist are songs you just want played during the party or on the dance floor. It's always great to have at least one group line dance song, for example, the Electric Slide, Cupid Shuffle, or Macarena.

Party Favors

Your party favor is a memento from your reception. Many couples like to customize their favors with the wedding date or romantic sayings.

Destination Party Favor Ideas:

- Goodie bags filled with sweets and treats.

- Flowers (usually the decor/centerpieces are given after the party is over)

- Seashells with customization are great for beach weddings.

- A local treat native to the destination (coffee beans, nuts, jams, spices, etc.)

Location for Gifts

It is a priceless gift that your guests have extensively traveled to share such a joyous occasion in your life. Don't expect a million tangible gifts; however be prepared and have an envelope box and small table available for gifts from guests.

Honeymoon

This is the one part of the entire ceremony of events that is solely about you and your mate. Honeymooning is a time for adventure, relaxing, and celebrating your new commitment to one another. All the high emotions, anxiety, and stress are over and it's time to just enjoy one another.

Having a Fabulous Destination Wedding makes honeymooning simple yet luxurious. By choosing to have a FDW, you are already at your honeymoon destination! You immediately get to relax and enjoy yourselves without the hassle of flying out to your honeymoon destination.

FDW Tip: The FDW team highly recommends upgrading to a Presidential or Honeymoon suite, if you don't already have one of the best rooms. Also, move your packed belongings to the upgraded room before the ceremony. It's a nice treat to end your big day in an upgraded room with your mate and not worry about changing rooms after the ceremony.

Your honeymoon should consist of a flexible plan. Many hotels have a travel representative on site to plan any of your excursion or adventure needs. The FDW team recommends that you do some pre-planning of possible excursions, with a

list of possible back up options. Some excursions are weather permitting and you wouldn't want to waste a full day figuring out the next plan. By pre-planning your excursions, you get to design your perfect honeymoon and ensure that it is budget-friendly. Also, be sure to check out the hotspots included in the destination chapters 3 – 9.

Here's a list of fun honeymoon activity options

- Couple's massage

- Local excursions (ziplining, hiking, museum visit, sightseeing)

- Water excursions (parasailing, kayaking, day cruise, snorkeling)

- Tours

- Shows / Concerts

- Brunch or Dinner Cruise / Dinner at sunset with an Ocean view

ENJOY!

Chapter 22 Traditions, T-shirts and Thank you's

The wedding is over. You had a Fabulous Destination Wedding on a shoestring budget...*A Fairy Tale Affair*!

Traditions

While you are blissfully sipping a tropical drink, happy to be honeymooning, think about starting your first family tradition as a couple. Traditions bind families from one generation to the next. It is something you can share as a couple. What will you want some of your family traditions to be? Family traditions ensure that the warmth and closeness of the family continues. Some traditions that are passed down to you, you will continue with your new family. But as a couple you may also want to start some new traditions.

You are on your honeymoon, so don't over-reflect about family traditions. Many couples start new traditions on their honeymoon, without even knowing it. Some couples use this opportunity to start a collection of destination family photo frames, or holiday ornaments, or whatever you fancy. This is a fun tradition and you will never be honeymooning again, in this locale, so go for it; start a crazy souvenir collection!

> **FDW Tip:** The best souvenirs tend to be a reminder of your time spent at that destination, is somewhat unique to that locale, and also has some utilitarian value; even artwork has a utilitarian purpose. Avoid souvenirs that end up being junk, that's thrown away in a couple of years when you are de-cluttering. Quality souvenirs with personal meaning and good craftsmanship hold the test of time.

T-shirts

T-shirts over the years have been given a bad rep as souvenirs. However, the FDW team likes quality t-shirts as souvenirs. T-shirts were given their name due to their shape, with the short sleeves forming the letter "T".

In 1913, the U.S. Navy began issuing them, and sailors would remove their outer shirts, exposing and soiling their t-shirt underneath. In the 1950's actor, Marlon Brando made them fashionable, outerwear garments after starring in the movie, "A Streetcar Named Desire." In the 1960's the t-shirt became a means of self-expression and advertisement. In the 1980's, the white tee became popular after actor Don Johnson began wearing them under Armani suits in "Miami Vice". Now, t-shirts are available in various styles, fabrics, and colors. It is the one wardrobe piece that most people own at least one.

When selecting a souvenir t-shirt, consider the quality of the fabric, uniqueness of the design and quality in the craftsmanship. Screen printed shirts do not hold up as well as embroidery designs when washed. However, the better artistic designs tend to be on screen-printed shirts, because the design capabilities are endless. Unless you find a really cool screen-printed shirt that speaks to you, go for an embroidered-decorated shirt.

When selecting a t-shirt also consider the fabric. 100% cotton jersey, and cotton/polyester blends are touted as the most comfortable fabrics for t-shirts. If you live in a warmer climate, t-shirts are very functional. However, if you live in a climate with four seasons, you may want to consider a sweatshirt collection.

Thank you's

Many bridal magazines and books advise sending thank-you notes immediately when you have received a wedding gift to avoid having to send them all at once. We at the FDW team suggest opening up your gifts and sending out thank-you notes within 30 days after you return from your honeymoon. Shipped gifts should be immediately acknowledged, so that the sender knows that you did receive it, however they do not need to be opened up at that time. Be sure to follow up with a thank-you note specifically mentioning the gift when you send out your other thank-you notes.

Unless someone wants you to open their gift in advance, save the opening of gifts until after you return. This gives you something else to look forward to when the honeymoon is over. After all, who looks forward to leaving an exotic destination, sipping Mai Tai's or Bahama Mama's?

FDW Tip: Pre-schedule a gift opening and thank-you writing day into your wedding activities to-do list. Give it the same importance as your pre-wedding activities to ensure that it is not delayed.

Personalize all thank-you notes. Every guest that attended your FDW should receive a personal thank-you note, if they gave you a tangible gift or not. Everyone that attended your FDW did something that made your wedding extra-special. In addition to thanking them for their gift; thank them for attending and how they made your day extra special in the thank-you note.

Lastly, remember to send thank-you letters to your suppliers, vendors, resort/hotel personnel and other professionals. When you send thank-you letters to these professionals, be sure to copy the next-level of management, as appropriate. They will appreciate the additional recognition.

The wedding is over, your thank-you notes and letters are in the mail, so now what? You begin your next chapter!

Disclaimer: The FDW team has made every effort to provide you with information that is accurate and current. Because marriage license requirements, companies, and other information presented is subject to change, the authors make no guarantees regarding the information provided in this book. Also, although we offer general information for getting married in various destinations, you will need to research the requirements of your home country and selected destination for the current requirements, laws and regulations.

Directory and Resources

This directory is just a short list of resources to assist you in your wedding planning research.

All-Inclusive Resorts and Hotels

Bahia Principe	www.bahia-principe.com
Couples	www.couples.com
Dreams	www.dreamsresorts.com
Excellence	www.excellence-resorts.com
Grand Palladium	www.palladiumhotelgroup.com
Iberostar	www.iberostar.com
Majestic Colonial	www.majestic-resorts.com
Occidental	www.occidentalhotels.com
Paradisus	www.paradisus.com/
Riu	www.riu.com
Sandals	www.sandals.com
Secrets	www.secretsresorts.com/

Tourism Boards

Jamaica	www.visitjamaica.com
Dominican Republic	www.godominicanrepublic.com
Mexico	www.visitmexico.com
Bahamas	www.bahamas.com
Saint Lucia	www.stlucianow.com
Costa Rica	www.visitcostarica.com
Las Vegas	www.lasvegas.com

Passport Application and Travel Information

U.S. Department of State
http://travel.state.gov/content/passports/english.html

Smart Traveler Enrollment Program
http://travel.state.gov/content/passports/english/go/step.html

Information on Getting Married Abroad
http://travel.state.gov/content/passports/english/abroad/events-and-ecords/marriage.html

Travel Resources and Websites

http://www.applevacations.com/

www.booking.com/

www.cheapoair.com/

www.expedia.com/

www.fodors.com/

www.hotels.com/

www.hotwire.com/

www.kayak.com/

www.orbitz.com/

www.priceline.com

www.travelocity.com/

www.travelzoo.com/

www.tripadvisor.com/

www.vacationstogo.com/

www.resortvacationstogo.com

www.resortvacationstogo.com/all-inclusive_resorts.html

Fabulous Destination Wedding
Worksheet

Top 3 destination choices:

1) _____

2) _____

3) _____

Top 3 Dates / Week choices:

1) _____

2) _____

3) _____

Top 3 Hotels / Resort choices:

1) _____

2) _____

3) _____

Passport:

1) Do you and your mate have valid passports? (If not, apply ASAP)

Yes _____ No _____

Your Fabulous Destination Wedding
Notes:

THANK YOU!

The FDW team wishes you all the best in planning your Fabulous Destination Wedding. We hope that this reference guide has provided you with information and details you will need in the upcoming months. Thank you for selecting *"A Fairy Tale Affair – How to Plan a Fabulous Destination Wedding on a Shoestring Budget"*, as one of your wedding planning resources.

About the Authors:

Deborah McKenzie has worked in Corporate America for most of her career. In her various positions, she has written articles for several professional journals and drafted instruction and training manuals. As a working woman, wife and mother of three, she constantly juggled with finding the right balance between work and family. When her kids became adults, she finally was able to achieve that balance. She lives in Fort Worth, Texas with her husband of 30 years and is transitioning to a career as a full-time writer. She writes on topics of interest to women, children and families.

Danielle Wigfall resides in Southern California with her husband, Tyson. She has performed in film and on stage around the country and overseas. When not acting, Danielle plans special events, including weddings. Danielle blogs on topics of interest to young couples and young adults. She can be reached through her website at www.crinlo.com.

The book cover was designed by **Tyson Wigfall**. In addition to his position in Marketing, Tyson is a graphic designer and website developer. For projects, he can also be reached through www.crinlo.com.

Interior technical formatting was coded by **Lee Reed, III**. For projects, he can be reached at leereed7@gmail.com.

The models were photographed in Montego Bay, Jamaica.

Made in the USA
San Bernardino, CA
29 May 2014